Instructor's Manual

to accompany

Cases

for use with

Foundations of Financial Management

Eleventh Edition

Stanley B. Block
Texas Christian University

Geoffrey A. Hirt
DePaul University

Instructor's Manual to accompany Cases for use with
FOUNDATIONS OF FINANCIAL MANAGEMENT
Stanley B. Block and Geoffrey A. Hirt

Published by McGraw-Hill/Irwin, an imprint of The McGraw-Hill Companies, Inc., 1221 Avenue of the Americas, New York, NY 10020. Copyright © 2005, 2002, 2000, 1996, 1994, 1992, 1989, 1987, 1984, 1981, 1978 by The McGraw-Hill Companies, Inc. All rights reserved.
The contents, or parts thereof, may be reproduced in print form solely for classroom use with
FOUNDATIONS OF FINANCIAL MANAGEMENT
provided such reproductions bear copyright notice, but may not be reproduced in any other form or for any other purpose without the prior written consent of The McGraw-Hill Companies, Inc., including, but not limited to, in any network or other electronic storage or transmission, or broadcast for distance learning.

1 2 3 4 5 6 7 8 9 0 QSR/QSR 0 9 8 7 6 5 4

ISBN 0-07-284237-7

www.mhhe.com

Contents

Case

1. Harrod's Sporting Goods 1
2. Chem-Med Company 4
3. Glen Mount Furniture Company 7
4. Genuine Motor Products 11
5. Gale Force Surfing 15
6. Modern Kitchenware Co. 21
7. Fresh & Fruity Foods, Inc. 25
8. Pierce Control Systems 29
9. Allison Boone, M.D. 33
10. Billy Wilson—All American 38
11. Gilbert Enterprises 41
12. Berkshire Instruments 45
13. Galaxy Systems, Inc. 49
14. Aerocomp, Inc. 53
15. Phelps Toy Company 56
16. Inca, Inc. 59
17. Robert Boyle & Associates, Inc. 62
18. Leland Industries 65
19. Warner Motor Oil Company 69
20. Midsouth Exploration Company 73
21. Alpha Biogenetics 76
22. Montgomery Corporation 79
23. Orbit Chemical Company 82
24. Hamilton Products 85
25. Security Software, Inc. 87
26. National Brands vs. A-1 Holdings 90
27. KFC and the Colonel 94

Harrod's Sporting Goods

Case 1

Ratio Analysis

Purpose: The case allows the student to examine ratio analysis within the context of a customer-banking arrangement. The firm has a disagreement with the bank over how much it should be paying in relation to prime (no prior knowledge of banking is required for the case). An item of particular interest is the impact of an extraordinary loss on the firm's income statement. It has a major effect on the analysis of the company. Industry comparisons also are utilized.

Relation to Text: The case should follow Chapter 3.

Complexity: The case is moderately complex. It should require a to 1½ hours.

Solutions

1. Ratios

		2001	2002	2003
1.	$\dfrac{\text{Net income}}{\text{Sales}}$	4.522	5.42%	3.99%
2a.	$\dfrac{\text{Net income}}{\text{Total assets}}$	6.09%	7.23%	5.71%
b.	Net income sales x sales / total assets	4.52 x 1.35	5.42% x 1.33	3.99% x 1.43
3a.	$\dfrac{\text{Net income}}{\text{Stockholder's equity}}$	16.04%	18.55%	15.02%
b.	$\dfrac{\text{Net income / total assets}}{(1 - \text{debt / total assets})}$	$\dfrac{6.09\%}{(1-.620)}$	$\dfrac{7.23\%}{(1-.610)}$	$\dfrac{5.71\%}{(1-.620)}$

2. Harrod's has suffered a sharp decline in its profit margin, particularly between 2002 and 2003 (5.42% down to 3.99%). Return on assets is also down, but not quite as much due to a slight increase in asset turnover. Return on stockholders' equity is also down.

3.

		2001	2002	2003
1.	$\dfrac{\text{Net income}}{\text{Sales}}$	4.522	5.42%	**6.19%**
2a.	$\dfrac{\text{Net income}}{\text{Total assets}}$	6.09%	7.23%	**8.85%**
2b.	Net income sales x sales / total assets	4.52 x 1.35	5.42% x 1.33	**6.19% x 1.43**
3a.	$\dfrac{\text{Net income}}{\text{Stockholder's equity}}$	16.04%	18.55%	**23.30%**
3b.	$\dfrac{\text{Net income / total assets}}{(1 - \text{debt / total assets})}$	$\dfrac{6.09\%}{(1-.620)}$	$\dfrac{7.23\%}{(1-.610)}$	$\dfrac{\mathbf{8.85\%}}{\mathbf{(1-.620)}}$

4. After eliminating the effect of the nonrecurring extraordinary loss, the trend is clearly up over all three years. Particularly impressive is the increase in return on stockholders' equity from 16.04% in 2001 to 23.30% in 2003.

5. Harrod has a clear superiority in the profit margin (6.19% vs. 4.51%). This is further enhanced by a more rapid asset turnover (1.43 to 1.33) to give an even more superior return on total assets (8.85% vs. 5.1%). Finally, return on stockholders' equity greatly benefits from a higher debt ratio (62% vs. 48%) to provide an even larger gap between the firm and the industry (23.30% vs. 9.80%). While debt is not necessarily good, it has hiked up the return on equity to well over twice the industry figure.

6. | Ratios | | 2003 | Industry |
   |---|---|---|---|
   | 4. | Sales / Receivables | 7.35 | 6.75 |
   | 6. | Sales / Inventory | 4.75 | 3.01 |
   | 7. | Sales / Fixed assets | 2.77 | 3.20 |

   Harrod's is clearly superior to the industry in receivables turnover (7.35 vs. 6.75) and inventory turnover (4.75 vs. 3.01) and this more than compensates for a lower sales to fixed assets ratio (2.77 vs. 3.20).

7. Becky would appear to have strong grounds for a complaint. It appears that the banker was using unadjusted income statement numbers to arrive at the conclusion that Harrod's was on a downward trend in terms of the profitability ratios. Also, using unadjusted data the profit margin was below the industry average.

   However, the inferior performance was due to an extraordinary, nonrecurring loss. In terms of normal operating performance, the company is clearly on an upward trend and well above the industry averages on all counts. One percent over prime appears to be much more reasonable than 2½ percent over prime.

Chem-Med Company

Case 2

Ratio Analysis

Purpose: The case allows the student to go into financial analyses in more depth than in possible with end-of-chapter problems. In addition to computing a series of ratios, the student must consider industry data and trends for the purpose of evaluating relative performance. The student must also make use of the Du Pont system of analysis. Of special interest are the debt and performance covenants established by the potential financier. Finally, the student is forced to identify the impact of extraordinary income on ratio analysis and how it can distort one year's performance.

Relation to Text: The case should follow Chapter 3.

Complexity: The case is moderately complex. It should require 1-1½ hours.

Solutions

1. Sales Growth = (Sales this year − Sales last year) / Sales last year
    for 2003 $ 3,814 − $3,051 / $3,051 = + 25%
    for 2004   5,340 − 3,814 / 3,814 = + 40%
    for 2005   7,475 − 5,340 / 5,340 = + 40%
    for 2006   10,466 − 7,475 / 7,475 = + 40%

2. Net income growth = (Net income this year − Net income last year) / Net Income last year
    for 2004 $1,609 − $1,150 / $1,150 = + 40%
    for 2005   1,943 − 1,609 / 1,609 = + 21%
    for 2006   2,903 − 1,943 / 1,943 = + 49%

According to Dr. Swan's estimates net income growth will match sales growth in 2004, then slack off and rebound in 2006. However, Dr. Swan's figures are misleading: in 2004 they include $500,000 worth of extraordinary income expected to be received from the settlement of the suit with Pharmacia. The astute analyst will realize that this amount should be excluded from his/her calculations because (1) receiving the amount is by no means certain, and (2) it is a one-time event which has nothing to do with the operations of the company. When the amount is excluded from 2004's figures we see that net income growth for 2004 is actually considerably less than 40%.

Aftertax effect of removing $500,000 from gross income = $500 x (1 − tax rate) = $500 x (1 − .33) = − $355

New net income = $1,609 − $335 = $1,274
Appropriate net income growth for 1999   = ($1,274 − $1,150) / $1,150
                                                                           = + 11%

Failing to exclude the extraordinary amount has the effect of obscuring the "real" profitability ratios—ROE in 2002 would be 23%, not 29%. Net profit margin would be 24%, not 30%. These are facts a potential investor would want to know.

3. Chem-Med's current ratio = Current Assets / Current Liabilities:
    for 2003 = $1,720 / $ 593 = 2.90
    for 2006 = $3,261 / $1,647 = 1.98

Pharmacia had a current ratio in 2003 of 2.8, and the industry average was 2.4. Chem-Med, therefore, in 2003 was slightly more liquid than the average company. This would probably be looked upon favorably by someone considering loaning money to the company; however, the banker with whom Dr. Swan had lunch would have a problem with Chem-Med's current ratio for 2006: it falls below the 2.25 to 1 limit he would establish as a restrictive covenant. In view of that, Dr. Swan needs to revise his financial plan for 2006 in such a way that less money is invested in fixed assets, and more is held in cash & equivalents (or, alternatively, shift some current liabilities to long-term debt and/or equity).

4. Chem-Med's total debt to assets ratio = total liabilities / total assets
    for 2003 = $ 614 / $ 4,491 = .137
    for 2004 = $ 857 / $ 6,343 = .135
    for 2005 = $1,212 / $ 8,641 = .140
    for 2006 = $1,664 / $11,995 = .139

The variation from year to year is small—no trend can be established, except, of course, that the ratio remains nearly constant, indicating that Chem-Med is doing a good job in managing its debt. It was doing especially well in 2003 compared to other companies in the industry, where the average debt to assets ratio was .52 (and Pharmacia's was .55). A potential investor in Chem-Med's stock might be pleased or displeased depending on his/her tolerance for risk and outlook for the future. (Chem-Med has much less financial risk than average, but the company, which is in a growth situation, might be considered to be underleveraged.)

5. Chem-Med's average accounts receivable collection period = accounts receivable / sales per day

   for 2003 = $ 564 / ($ 3,814/360) = 53 days
   for 2004 = $ 907 / ($ 5,340/360) = 61 days
   for 2005 = $1,495 / ($ 7,475/360) = 72 days
   for 2006 = $2,351 / ($10,466/360) = 81 days

   This is not a good sign. The average length of time that Chem-Med's customers are taking to pay for products they've bought is increasing steadily every year. If Chem-Med's credit policy is, say, 2/10, net 30, it is clear that very few customers are adhering to it, and the situation is getting worse. Not only is Chem-Med, in effect, granting fee credit to those customers by allowing them to delay payment for so long, it is paying for such credit itself. The company's higher balances of accounts receivable must be financed in some way, either through additional debt or equity, and these additions have a cost.

6. Chem-Med's return on equity ratio = net income / total equity for 1998 = $1,150 / $3,877 = 29.6%

   Pharmacie's ROE in 2003 was 29.6%, and the industry average was only 12.3%. A potential investor in Chem-Med would be very pleased; Chem-Med is offering a handsome return that's almost two and a half times that of the average company in the industry. Now, the investor will want to use the Du Pont method to look further at Chem-Med and Pharmacia to determine the source of this return.

	ROE	=	Profit Margin	x	Asset Turnover	/	(1 – Debt to Assets)
Chem-Med, 2000	.2970	=	.3015	x	.85	/	(1 – .137)
Pharmacia:	.2956	=	.07	x	1.9	/	(1 – .55)

   Note the drastic difference in the operation of the two companies, even though their ROEs are nearly the same. Chem-Med makes relatively few sales (low asset turnover), but makes a lot of money on each one (30%). Pharmacia is just the opposite: it makes a lot of sales, and only a little profit (7%) on each one. Pharmacia's ROE is also being propped up by greater use of debt than Chem-Med (Pharmacia has relatively less equity; so the same amount of income will represent a greater return to Pharmacia's equity holders than Chem-Med's). All other considerations being equal, a potential investor would probably prefer Chem-Med's position, but it's by no means certain (for example, it's much more serious for Chem-Med to lose a sale).

Glen Mount Furniture Company   Case 3

Financial Leverage

Purpose: The potential impact of changes in the debt level on earnings per share is the central focus of the case. However, the instructor can derive educational benefits that go well beyond this point. The central figure in the case is frustrated by security analyst's short-term emphasis on earnings per share and their lack of concern for the long-term fundamentals associated with his firm. This rather common situation can be drawn upon to make for a more dynamic discussion process. The student is given ample opportunities to calculate EPS under different financial leverage strategies and to examine debt ratios, and degrees of leverage.

Relation to Text: The case should follow Chapter 5. Because the case has some elementary valuation considerations as well, it also could be used later in the course.

Complexity: The case is moderately complex. It should require 1 hour.

Solutions

1. | | |
    |---|---:|
    | Sales ($45,500,000 + $500,000) | $45,500,000 |
    | Fixed costs | 12,900,000 |
    | Variable costs (58% of sales) | 26,390,000 |
    | Operating income (EBIT) | 6,210,000 |
    | Interest | 1,275,000 |
    | Earnings before taxes (EBT) | 4,935,000 |
    | Taxes (34%) | 1,677,000 |
    | Earnings after taxes (EAT) | 3,257,100 |
    | Shares | 2,000,000 |
    | Earnings per share | $1.63 |

2. | | |
    |---|---:|
    | Earnings per share, 2005 | $1.63 |
    | Earnings per share, 2004 | 1.56 |
    | Increase | $ .07 |

    $$\frac{\text{Increase}}{\text{Earnings per share, 2004}} = \frac{\$.07}{1.56} = 4.5\%$$

3. | | |
    |---|---:|
    | Sales | $45,500,000 |
    | Fixed costs | 12,900,000 |
    | Variable costs (58% of sales) | 26,390,000 |
    | Operating income (EBIT) | 6,210,000 |
    | Interest* | 2,400,000 |
    | Earnings before taxes (EBT) | 3,810,000 |
    | Taxes (34%) | 1,295,000 |
    | Earnings after taxes (EAT) | 2,514,600 |
    | Shares** | 1,375,000 |
    | Earnings per share | $1.83 |

    *Interest
    Old debt 10.625% x $12,000,000 = $1,275,000
    New debt 11.250% x $10,000,000 = 1,125,000
    Total interest $2,400,000

    **Shares outstanding 2,000,000 – 625,000 = 1,375,000

4. | | |
    |---|---:|
    | Earnings per share, 2005 (based on more debt) | $1.83 |
    | Earnings per share, 2004 | 1.56 |
    | | $ .27 |

    $$\frac{\text{Increase}}{\text{Earnings per share, 2004}} \quad \frac{\$.27}{\$1.56} = 17.3\%$$

5. $$\text{DFL}(1) = \frac{\text{EBIT}}{\text{EBIT} - \text{I}} = \frac{\$6,210,000}{\$6,210,000 - \$1,275,000} = \frac{\$6,210,000}{\$4,935,000} = 1.26$$

$$\text{DFL}(3) = \frac{\text{EBIT}}{\text{EBIT} - \text{I}} = \frac{\$6,210,000}{\$6,210,000 - \$2,400,000} =$$

$$= \frac{\$6,210,000}{\$3,810,000} = 1.63$$

6. $$\text{DCL}(1) = \frac{\text{S} - \text{TVC}}{\text{S} - \text{TVC} - \text{FC} - \text{I}}$$

$$= \frac{\$45,500,000 - \$26,390,000}{\$45,500,000 - \$26,390,000 - \$12,900,000 - \$1,275,000}$$

$$= \frac{\$19,110,000}{\$\ 4,935,000} = 3.87$$

$$\text{DCL}(3) = \frac{\text{S} - \text{TVC}}{\text{S} - \text{TVC} - \text{FC} - \text{I}}$$

$$= \frac{\$45,500,000 - \$26,390,000}{\$45,500,000 - \$26,930,000 - \$12,900,000 - \$2,400,000}$$

$$= \frac{\$19,110,000}{\$\ 3,810,000} = 5.02$$

7. From Figure 2:
$$\frac{\text{Total debt}}{\text{Total assets}} = \frac{\$17,500,000}{\$40,500,000} = 43.2\%$$
After new debt issue:
$$\frac{\text{Total debt}}{\text{Total assets}} = \frac{\$17,500,000 + \$10,000,000}{\$40,500,000} = \frac{\$27,500,000}{\$40,500,000} = 67.9\%$$

8. There are two conflicting factors that could influence the stock price.

On the positive side, earnings per share would be twenty cents higher with more debt ($1.83 versus $1.63).

Based on a current price-earnings ratio of about 10 (the repurchase price for the shares is for $16 ($10,000,000 / 625,000) and EPS are currently $1.56), the stock might go up by approximately $2.00 as a result of a $.20 increase in EPS.

Two dollars represents a healthy 12.5% increase from the current value of $16 per share. However, the student must keep in mind that the debt ratio is increasing from 43.2% to 67.9%, which probably would have a negative effect on the price-earnings ratio.

The net effect of the increase in earnings per share versus the likely decrease in the price-earnings ratio can only be conjectured. Security analysts following Glen Mount Furniture Company seem to be highly sensitive to earnings per share performance, but there may be some question about whether the type of financial engineering used to increase the earnings per share will satisfy them. Of course, the firm can argue that the share repurchase is a strong sign of confidence by management in future company performances.

One clue to the eventual reaction of the market to the recapitalization might lie in the data on the debt ratios of other firms in the industry. If 67.9% is perceived to be on the high end, there might be little positive gain associated with the increase in earnings per share. However, if other companies are in this range and the firm is merely taking advantage of underutilitzed debt capacity, the market reaction might be positive.

Genuine Motor Products Case 4

Combined Leverage

Purpose: The case illustrates the potential impact on a company when it goes from dependence on labor intensive variable costs to fixed cost automation. The effects are further highlighted when the new equipment is heavily financed by debt. The upside is emphasized through increased earnings per share, while the downside is related to a higher break-even level (an expanded definition of cash flow break-even is introduced and very carefully explained). Not only are earnings per share and break-even covered, but so are all the various measures of degree of leverage. In addition to numerous calculations, the student is called upon to make judgmental decisions as an aggressive industrial engineer comes into conflict with a conservative chief financial officer.

Relation to Text: The case should follow Chapter 5.

Complexity: The case is moderately complex. It should require 1 – 1½ hours.

Solutions

1.   Figure 4

Sales (1,000,000 units @ $30 per unit)... $30,000,000
   Fixed costs*.. 5,800,000
   Total variable costs (1,000,000 units @ $18.80 per unit)............................. 18,800,000
Operating income (EBIT)... 5,400,000
   Interest (10.75% x $12,000,000)... 1,290,000
Earnings before taxes... 4,110,000
   Taxes (35%).. 1,438,500
Earnings after taxes.. 2,671,500
Shares... 2,320,000
Earnings per share.. $1.15

*Fixed costs include $2,800,000 in depreciation.

2. The first reason earnings per share has increased from $.91 to $1.15 relates to automation. That is even though fixed costs have gone up, total variable costs have gone down by even more. Thus, automation has lead to an increase in operating income from $3,000,000 to $5,400,000. This first reason relates to the use of operating leverage.

A second reason is that the $14 million increase in fixed assets was heavily financed by debt rather than equity. Out of $14 million of new financing, $10 million was in debt and only $4 million in new stock. The second reason relates to the use of financial leverage.

3.
$$DOL = \frac{Q(P-VC)}{Q(P-VC)-FC}$$

Before (Figure 2)

$$\frac{1{,}000{,}000(\$30-\$25)}{1{,}000{,}000(\$30-\$25)-\$2{,}000{,}000}$$

$$=\frac{1{,}000{,}000(\$5)}{1{,}000{,}000(\$5)-2{,}000{,}000}$$

$$=\frac{\$5{,}00{,}000}{\$3{,}000{,}000}=1.67$$

After (Figure 4)

$$\frac{1{,}000{,}000(\$30-\$18.80)}{1{,}000{,}000(\$30-\$18.80)-\$5{,}800{,}000}$$

$$\frac{1{,}000{,}000(\$11.20)}{1{,}000{,}000(\$11.20)-\$5{,}800{,}000}$$

$$\frac{\$11{,}200{,}000}{5{,}400{,}000}=2.07$$

$$DFL = \frac{EBIT}{EBIT-I}$$

Before (Figure 2)	After (Figure 4)
$$\frac{\$3,000,000}{\$3,000,000-\$215,000}$$	$$\frac{\$5,400,000}{\$5,400,000-\$1,290,000}$$
$$=\frac{\$3,000,000}{\$2,785,000}=1.08$$	$$=\frac{\$5,400,000}{4,110,000}=1.31$$

$$DCL = \frac{Q(P-VC)}{Q(P-VC)-FC-I}$$

Before (Figure 2)	After (Figure 4)
$$\frac{1,000,000\,(\$30-\$25)}{1,000,000\,(\$30-\$25)-\$2,000,000-\$215,000}$$	$$\frac{1,000,000\,(\$30-\$18.80)}{1,000,000\,(\$30-\$18.80)-\$5,800,000-\$1,290,000}$$
$$=\frac{1,000,000\,(\$5)}{1,000,000\,(\$5)-\$2,215,000}$$	$$\frac{1,000,000\,(\$11.20)}{1,000,000\,(\$11.20)-\$7,090,000}$$
$$=\frac{\$5,000,000}{\$2,785,000}=1.80$$	$$=\frac{\$11,200,000}{4,110,000}=2.73$$

4.

$$BE = \frac{FC}{P-VC}$$

Before (Figure 2)	After (Figure 4)
$$\frac{\$2,000,000}{\$30-\$25}$$	$$\frac{\$5,800,000}{\$30-\$18.80}$$
$$\frac{\$2,000,000}{\$5}=400,000 \text{ units}$$	$$\frac{\$5,800,000}{\$11.20}=517,857 \text{ units}$$

5. Revised BE = $\dfrac{\text{(Fixed costs - Depreciation)} + \text{Interest}}{\text{Price (P) - (VC) Variable cost per unit}}$

Before (Figure 2)   After (Figure 4)

$$\dfrac{(\$2{,}000{,}000 - \$1{,}000{,}000) + \$215{,}000}{\$30 - \$25} \qquad \dfrac{(\$5{,}800{,}000 - \$2{,}800{,}000) + 1{,}290{,}000}{\$30 - \$18.80}$$

$$= \dfrac{1{,}000{,}000 + \$215{,}000}{\$5} \qquad\qquad = \dfrac{\$3{,}000{,}000 + \$1{,}290{,}000}{\$11.20}$$

$$= \dfrac{\$1{,}215{,}000}{\$5} = 243{,}000 \text{ units} \qquad = \dfrac{\$4{,}290{,}000}{\$11.20} = 383{,}036 \text{ units}$$

6. Using the revised break-even analysis from question 5, the company would be in trouble. It requires 383,036 units to cover all cash outflows, and at 300,000 units, this is not possible. While 300,000 units represents only 30 percent of current sales volume of 1,000,000 units, the auto parts industry is highly cyclical.

7. Earnings per share at 1,500,000 units

Sales (1,500,000 units @ $30 per unit)	$45,000,000
Fixed costs	5,800,000
Total variable costs (1,500,000 units @ $18.80 per unit)	28,200,000
Operating income	11,000,000
Interest (10.75% x $12,000,000)	1,290,000
Earnings before taxes	9,710,000
Taxes (35%)	3,398,500
Earnings after taxes	$ 6,311,500
Shares	2,320,000
Earnings per share	$2.72

8. There is no correct answer as to who is right. The changes that Mike Anton suggests will definitely increase profitability. At 1,000,000 units, earnings per share are $.91 under the old plan and $1.15 under the new plan. At 1,500,000 units, the gap is even wider. Earnings per share are $1.72 under the old plan and $2.72 under the new plan.

On the other hand, the new plan exposes the firm to more risk of not covering its cash obligations. As computed in question 6, the revised break-even point is 383,036 units under the new plan and a somewhat safer 243,000 units under the old plan. For example, at a volume of 300,000 units, the company could meet its cash obligations under the old plan, but not under the new plan.

The key variable in determining the success or failure of the new plan is volume. As long as volume stays the same or goes up, the new plan is definitely going to be a success (even if volume declines somewhat, it may still be desirable). However, if volume falls sharply in a recession, the new plan could be a failure. As is almost always true with leverage, volume is quite important in determining success or failure.

Gale Force Surfing

Case 5

Working Capital—Level vs. Seasonal Production

Purpose: The case forces the student to view the impact of level versus seasonal production on inventory levels, bank loan requirements, and profitability. It also considers the efficiencies (or inefficiencies) covered by the different production plans. The computations in the case are parallel to Table 6-1 through Table 6-5 in the text, with the only difference being that seasonal production rather than level production is being utilized. The case allows the student to properly track the movement of cash flow through the production process.

Relation to Text: The case should follow Chapter 6.

Complexity: The case involves numerous computations and may require 2 hours.

Solutions

1. New Tables 1 through 5, with Tim's suggestion implemented, are shown in the following pages. Observe that the inventory level is now constant at 400 units or $800,000 a month because all units produced are sold. As a side point, note that there may be no apparent need now to maintain the 400 units a month in inventory that were on hand at the start of the cycle. The inventory level could be reduced to the level that management feels would be sufficient to cover emergencies (or maybe to zero, which is what the Japanese do in a "just-in-time" production concept).

   Though not required, you may wish to refer to the old and new Table 4 to make a special point. Note that Tim's suggestion causes inventory balances to decrease over the time period and total current assets to fluctuate less, but the same balances occur at the end of September for inventory and total current assets.

2. New Table 5 shows the new cumulative loan balances and the interest expenses incurred each month. Under the old system (level production), total interest expense (at 1% a month on the cumulative loan balance) was $254,250. Under the proposed system it decreases to $50,750 for a savings of $203,500.

3. The first step is to compute total sales. Using the second row of Table 3 (either the old or new table), the total is $14,400,000. With an added expense burden of .5%, expenses will go up by $72,000. This is still far less than the interest savings of $203,500 computed in question 2, so the seasonal production plan is justified.

Interest savings...................................	$203,500
Added production expense................	72,000
Net savings..	$131,500

Note: Values are assumed to be computed on a pretax basis.

GALE FORCE SURFING (With Tim's suggestion implemented)

TABLE 1. SALES FORECAST (in units)

1st Quarter		2nd Quarter		3rd Quarter		4th Quarter	
October	150	January	0	April	500	July	1,000
November	75	February	0	May	1,000	August	500
December	25	March	300	June	1,000	September	250

TABLE 2. PRODUCTION SCHEDULE AND INVENTORY (seasonal production)

	Beginning Inventory	Production this Month	Sales	Ending Inventory	Inventory ($2,000 per unit)
October	400	150	150	400	$800,000
November	400	75	75	400	$800,000
December	400	25	25	400	$800,000
January	400	0	0	400	$800,000
February	400	0	0	400	$800,000
March	400	300	300	400	$800,000
April	400	500	500	400	$800,000
May	400	1,000	1,000	400	$800,000
June	400	1,000	1,000	400	$800,000
July	400	1,000	1,000	400	$800,000
August	400	500	500	400	$800,000
September	400	250	250	400	$800,000

TABLE 3. SALES FORECAST, CASH RECEIPTS AND PAYMENTS, AND CASH BUDGET

	October	November	December	January	February	March	April
	Sales Forecast						
Sales (units)	150	75	25	0	0	300	500
Sales (unit price: $3,000)	$450,000	$225,000	$75,000	$0	$0	$900,000	$1,500,000
	Cash Receipts Schedule						
50% cash	$225,000	$112,500	$ 37,500	$ 0	$0	$450,000	$ 750,000
50% from prior month's sales	$375,000	$225,000	$112,500	$37,500	$0	$ 0	$ 450,000
Total Cash Receipts	$600,000	$337,500	$150,000	$37,500	$0	$ 0	$1,200,000
(Note: Sept. sales assumed to be $750,000)							
	Cash Payments Schedule						
Production in Units	150	75	25	0	0	300	500
Production Costs (each = $2,000)	$300,000	$150,000	$ 50,000	$ 0	$ 0	$600,000	$1,000,000
Overhead	$200,000	$200,000	$200,000	$200,000	$200,000	$200,000	$ 200,000
Dividends and Interest							
Taxes	$150,000			$150,000			$ 150,000
Total Cash Payments	$650,000	$350,000	$250,000	$350,000	$200,000	$800,000	$1,350,000
	Cash Budget—Required Minimum Balance is $125,000						
Cash Flow	$ −50,000	$ −12,000	$−100,000	$−312,500	$−200,000	$−350,000	$ −150,000
Beginning Cash	125,000	125,000	125,000	125,000	125,000	125,000	125,000
Cumulative Cash Balance	$ 75,000	$112,500	$ 25,000	$−187,500	$ −75,000	$−225,000	$ −25,000
Monthly Loan or (Repayment)	$ 50,000	$ 12,500	$ 100,000	$ 312,500	$ 200,000	$ 350,000	$ 150,000
Cumulative Loan	$ 50,000	$ 62,500	162,500	$ 475,000	$ 675,000	$1,025,000	$1,175,000
Ending Cash Balance	$125,000	$125,000	$ 125,000	$ 125,000	$ 125,000	$ 125,000	$ 125,000

TABLE 3. (Continued)   SALES FORECAST, CASH RECEIPTS AND PAYMENTS, AND CASH BUDGET

	May	June	July	August	September
Sales Forecast					
Sales (units)	1,000	1,000	1,000	500	250
Sales (unit price: $3,000)	$3,000,000	$3,000,000	$3,000,000	$1,500,000	$750,000
Cash Receipts Schedule					
50% cash	$1,500,000	$1,500,000	$1,500,000	$ 750,000	$ 375,000
50% from prior month's sales	$ 750,000	$1,500,000	$1,500,000	$1,500,000	$ 750,000
Total Cash Receipts	$2,250,000	$3,000,000	$3,000,000	$2,250,000	$1,125,000
(Note: Sept. sales assumed to be $750,000)					
Cash Payments Schedule					
Production in Units	1,000	1,000	1,000	500	250
Production Costs (each = $2,000)	$2,000,000	$2,000,000	$2,000,000	$1,000,000	$500,000
Overhead	$ 200,000	$ 200,000	$ 200,000	$ 200,000	$200,000
Dividends and Interest				$1,000,000	
Taxes			$ 300,000		
Total Cash Payments	$2,200,000	$2,200,000	$2,500,000	$2,200,000	$700,000
Cash Budget—Required Minimum Balance is $125,000					
Cash Flow	$ 50,000	$ 800,000	500,000	$ 500,000	$ 425,000
Beginning Cash	125,000	125,000	125,000	300,000	350,000
Cumulative Cash Balance	175,000	925,000	625,000	350,000	775,000
Monthly Loan or (Repayment)	$ (50,000)	$ (800,000)	$ (325,000)	$ 0	$ 0
Cumulative Loan	$ 1,125,000	$ 325,000	0	$ 0	$ 0
Ending Cash Balance	$ 125,000	$ 125,000	300,000	$ 350,000	$ 775,000

TABLE 4. TOTAL CURRENT ASSETS, FIRST YEAR

	Cash	Accounts* Receivable	Inventory	Total Current Assets
October	$125,000	$ 225,000	$800,000	$1,150,000
November	$125,000	$ 112,500	$800,000	$1,037,000
December	$125,000	$ 37,500	$800,000	$ 962,500
January	$125,000	$ 0	$800,000	$ 925,000
February	$125,000	$ 0	$800,000	$ 925,000
March	$125,000	$ 450,000	$800,000	$1,375,000
April	$125,000	$ 750,000	$800,000	$1,675,000
May	$125,000	$1,500,000	$800,000	$2,425,000
June	$125,000	$1,500,000	$800,000	$2,425,000
July	$300,000	$1,500,000	$800,000	$2,600,000
August	$350,000	$ 750,000	$800,000	$1,900,000
September	$775,000	$ 375,000	$800,000	$1,950,000

*Equals 50 percent of monthly sales

TABLE 5. CUMULATIVE LOAN BALANCE AND INTEREST EXPENSE (17% per month)

	October	November	December	January	February	March	April
Cumulative Loan Balance	$50,000	$62,500	$162,500	$475,000	$675,000	$1,025,000	$1,175,000
Interest Expense at 12.00% (Prime, 8.0%, + 4.0%)	$ 500	$ 625	$ 1,625	$ 4,750	$ 6,750	$ 10,250	$ 11,750

	May	June	July	August	September
Cumulative Loan Balance	$1,125,000	$ 325,000	$0	$0	$0
Interest Expense at 12.00% (Prime, 8.0%, + 4.0%)	$ 11,250	$ 3,250	$0	$0	$0

Total Interest Expense for the Year: $50,750

Modern Kitchenware Co.   Case 6

Cash Discount

Purpose: The case illustrates how the offering of a cash discount can affect the profitability of the firm. Three different cash discount policies are evaluated in terms of cost, freed up funds and the associated profitability. The impact of a cash discount on sales volume is also considered and has an impact on the final decision in the case.

Relation to Text: The case should follow Chapter 7.

Complexity: The case is moderately complex. It should require 1 hour.

Solutions

1.
Midpoint of Days Outstanding	Weights	Weighted Number of Days
5	.010	.050
15	.075	1.125
25	.200	5.000
35	.325	11.375
45	.215	9.675
55	.175	9.625
	1.000	36.850 Average Collection Period

2. **1/10, net 30 Policy**

10%	x	10	days	=	1	day
90%	x	30	days	=	27	days
					28	days Average Collection Period

2/10, net 30 Policy

25%	x	10	days	=	2.5	days
75%	x	30	days	=	22.5	days
					25.0	days Average Collection Period

3/10, net 30 Policy

60%	x	10	days	=	6	days
40%	x	30	days	=	12	days
					18	days Average Collection Period

3. Accounts receivable = average collection period x average daily credit sales

1/10, net 30 policy	28 days	x	$54,274	=	$1,519,672
2/10, net 30 policy	25 days	x	$54,274	=	$1,356,850
3/10, net 30 policy	18 days	x	$54,274	=	$976,932

It should be pointed out that if total credit sales billed remained the same under the three cash discount policies, average daily credit sales would go down due to the subtraction of the cash discount. However, for simplicity in the calculations, this point is not explicitly considered.

4. Cost of cash discount: Total credit sales x percent using the discount x % discount.

Cash Discount	Total Credit Sales		Percent Using the Discount		Percent Discount		Cost of Cash Discount
1/10, net 30 policy	$18,000,000	x	10%	x	1%	=	$ 18,000
2/10, net 30 policy	$18,000,000	x	25%	x	2%	=	$ 90,000
3/10, net 30 policy	$18,000,000	x	60%	x	3%	=	$324,000

5. Old accounts receivable – new accounts receivable = freed up funds

   1/10, net 30 policy
   $2,000,000 – $1,519,672 = $480,328

   2/10, net 30 policy
   $2,000,000 – $1,358,850 = $641,150

   3/10, net 30 policy
   $2,000,000 – $976,932 = $1,023,068

6. The return is equal to the freed up funds times 18%

1/10, net 30 policy	$ 480,328	x	18%	=	$ 86,459
2/10, net 30 policy	$ 641,150	x	18%	=	$115,407
3/10, net 30 policy	$1,023,068	x	18%	=	$184,152

7. Returns on freed up funds – cost of cash discounts = profit or loss

	Return on Freed up Funds		Cost of Cash Discount		Profit (loss)
1/10, net 30 policy	$ 86,459	–	$ 18,000	=	$ 68,459
2/10, net 30 policy	$115,407	–	$ 90,000	=	$ 25,407
3/10, net 30 policy	$184,152	–	$324,000	=	($139,848)

The 1/10, net 30 policy provides the largest profit.

8. Increased profitability of Alternative 2 (2/10, net 30) under the assumption of a $1,000,000 increase in sales.

Increased Sales	$1,000,000
Profit Margin	9%
Profit	$90,000
– Cost of cash discount (2% x $1,000,000)	20,000
– Lost profit on funds committed to accounts receivable (20% x $27,750)	5,550
Profit on new sales	$64,450
Previously computed Profit (Question 7)	25,407
Total profit on Alternative 2 (2/10, net 30)	$89,857

The total profit on Alternative 2 (2/10, net 30) of $89,857 now exceeds the profit of Alternative 1 (1/10, net 30) of $68,459 as computed in Question 7. The 2/10, net 30 policy should now be chosen.

Fresh & Fruity Foods, Inc. Case 7

Current-Asset Management

Purpose: The student must focus on accounts receivable as an investment (use of funds) and the financial advantages of reducing the commitment to this asset. At the same time the firm is also considering reductions to its accounts payable balance in order to take cash discounts. This alternative will call for additional bank financing, and comparative costs must be carefully assessed. The case utilizes many calculations that are covered in the text, but places them in a more complex, decision oriented framework.

Relation to Text: The case should follow the completion of Part Three (Working Capital) in the text. It primarily relies on material from chapters 7 and 8.

Complexity: The case is moderately complex. It should require 1-1½ hours.

Solutions

1. Average collection period = accounts receivable / average daily credit sales
   Accounts receivable   = $209,686
   Average daily credit sales = $1,179,000 / 360
                              = $3,275
   Average collection period = $209,686 / 3,275
                              = 64.03 days

2. Cost of failing to take a cash discount =

$$\frac{\text{Discount percent}}{100 \text{ percent} - \text{Discount percent}} \times \frac{360}{\text{Final due date} - \text{Discount percent}}$$

$$= \frac{2\%}{100\% - 2\%} \times \frac{360}{67 - 10}$$

$$= 2.04\% \times 6.32 = 12.89\%$$

The formula tells us that Fresh & Fruity is effectively paying 12.89% interest to delay paying the discounted amount for 57 days (the 67 days on which it pays less the 10 day discount period).

3. New accounts receivable = average collection period x average daily credit sales
   $104,800 = 32 x $3,275

Freed-up cash	=	Old accounts receivable	$209,686
	−	New accounts receivable	104,800
			$104,886
New accounts payable	=	Old accounts payable	$180,633
	−	Funds from accounts receivable	104,886
		New accounts payable	$ 75,747

4. Purchases (Figure 1) $969,000
   1/3 exposed to purchase discount 323,000
   2% purchase discount savings .... $ 6,460

   With the firm in a 33 percent tax bracket, a savings of $6,460 will produce $4,328 in aftertax income. The answer is equal to the cost savings x (1 – T)
   $6,460 (1 – .33) = $6,460 (.67) = $4,328

   This means total income will now be:
   Old income $50,623
   New aftertax income 4,328
   Total aftertax income $54,951

   Return on sales will be:

$$\frac{\text{Net income (after taxes)}}{\text{Sales}} = \frac{\$54,951}{\$1,179,000} = 4.66\%$$

This, of course, represents an improvement over the old figure of 4.29%.
Return on equity will be:

$$\frac{\text{Net income (after taxes)}}{\text{Equity}} = \frac{\$54,951}{\$123,600} = 44.46\%$$

This, also, represents an improvement over the old ratio of 40.96%. (Note: This firm has a particularly high return on equity because of rapid asset turnover and high current liabilities.) If the added profit is included in equity, the return is 42.95% ($54,951 / $127,928).

5. Accounts payable = average payment period x purchases per day

Average payment period	=	10 days
Purchases per day	=	[969,000 – (.02 x 969,000)] / 360
	=	($969,000 – $19,380) / 360
	=	$949,620 / 360
	=	$2,638
Accounts payable	=	10 x $2,638 = $26,380

Accounts payable from question 3 .... $75,747
Accounts payable from question 5 26,380
Size of bank loan required $49,367

This is the size of the bank loan required to take all cash discounts in 10 days.

6. The cost is the 8 percent interest on the bank loan of $49,367 or $3,949. The gain is the cash discounts taken of $19,380. The net gain before tax is $15,431 ($19,380 – $3,949).

On an aftertax basis this translates to a gain of $10,339 ($15,431 x .67).

7. First determine the amount of funds on which interest must be paid.

$49,367 – (.08 x $49,367) – (.20 x $49,367)
$49,367 – 3,949 – 9,874 = $35,544

Then divide the interest payment by this value.

$$\frac{\text{Interest}}{\text{Usable Funds}} = \frac{\$3,949}{\$35,544} = 11.10\%$$

The cost goes up from 8 percent to 11.10%. However, this value is still less than the cost of not taking the cash discount of 12.89% computed in question 2. Thus, it is advantageous to borrow and take the cash discount.

Note: Alert students may point out that Fresh & Fruity still needs $49,367 in cash no matter what kind of loan it is. Therefore, if the interest is to be charged on a discounted basis, and a compensating balance is required, Fresh & Fruity must borrow a larger amount to make up for it. Solve for the larger amount using algebra where L is the loan amount.

L – (.08 x L) – (.20 x L) = $49,367
L – .08L – .20L = $49,367
L – .28L = $49,367
.72L = $49,367
L = $49,367 / .72 = $68,565

Pierce Control Systems Case 8

Bank Financing

Purpose: The case allows the student to compare the cost of floating rate bank financing with longer-term fixed rate financing. The relative cost of each under different economic scenarios is considered and expected values are computed. There is also a brief consideration of the term structure of interest rates and the expectations of hypothesis. Another feature is that the student considers the trade-off between compensating balance requirements and lower quoted interest rates.

Relation to Text: The case draws on material from both Chapter 6 and Chapter 8 and should follow Chapter 8.

Complexity: This case is reasonably straightforward and requires 30-45 minutes to solve.

Pierce Control Systems

Solutions

1. Amount to be borrowed $= \dfrac{\text{Amount needed}}{(1-C)}$

    $= \dfrac{\$10,000,000}{(1-.1)}$

    $= \dfrac{\$10,000,000}{.9} = \$11,111,111$

2. $11,111,111   Loan requirement with compensating balance
   <u>   .055</u>   (prime rate minus 1/2%)
   $ 611,111   Interest cost on loan with compensating balance

   $10,000,000   Straight bank loan
   <u>x   .06</u>   Prime rate
   $ 600,000   Interest cost on straight bank loan

   The compensating balance loan would be more expensive.

3. $11,111,111   Compensating balance loan
   <u> 10,000,000</u>   Actual funds needed
   $ 1,111,111   Compensating balances
   <u>   4%</u>   Interest rate
   $ 44,444   Return on compensating balances

   $611,111   Interest cost on loan with compensating balance
   <u> –44,444</u>   Return on compensating balances
   $566,667   Net dollar interest cost of the compensating loan requirement

   The compensating balance loan would be less expensive than the 6% prime interest rate loan. ($566,667 vs. $600,000).

4. The term structure of interest rate curve is upward sloping. Under the expectations hypothesis, this would indicate that the next major move in interest rates is likely to be upward. Long-term rates reflect the average of expected short-term rates.

5. *Total interest cost with borrowing at prime over the next five years.*

Year	Amount	Interest Rate	Interest Cost
1994	$10,000,000	6%	$ 600,000
1995	10,000,000	8%	800,000
1996	10,000,000	9%	900,000
1997	10,000,000	9%	900,000
1998	10,000,000	4%	400,000
			$3,600,000

Total interest cost of the five year, 8% insurance company loan.

Amount	Interest Rate	Interest Cost	Years	Total Cost
$10,000,000	8%	$800,000	5	$4,000,000

The cost of the prime rate loan ($3,600,000) would be less than the five year insurance company loan ($4,000,000). Note the time value of money is not considered in this exercise.

6. *Total interest cost with borrowing at prime over the next five years (Second Scenario).*

Year	Amount	Interest Rate	Interest Cost
1994	$10,000,000	6%	$ 600,000
1995	10,000,000	10%	1,000,000
1996	10,000,000	15%	1,500,000
1997	10,000,000	13%	1,300,000
1998	10,000,000	13%	1,300,000
			$5,700,000

The cost of the prime rate loan ($5,700,000) would be greater than the five year insurance company loan ($4,000,000).

7. *Expected Value of Scenarios*

	Outcome	Probability	Expected Value
Scenario 1 (Question 5)	$3,600,000	.70	$2,520,000
Scenario 2 (Question 6)	5,700,000	.30	1,710,000
			$4,230,000

The expected value of dollar interest costs of short-term borrowing ($4,230,000) would be higher than the five year insurance company loan ($4,000,000).

8. Probability of the scenarios that produces an indifference point between short-term and long-term borrowing. Scenario 1 outcome (X) + Scenario 2 outcome (1–X) = Interest cost under long-term borrowing.

Note: X represents the probability of the outcome.
  Thus
$3,600,000X + $5,700,000 (1–X) = $4,000,000
$3,600,000X + $5,700,000 – $5,700,000X = $4,000,000
–$2,100,000X = –$1,700,000

$$X = \frac{-\$1,700,000}{-\$2,100,000} =$$

X = 80.95%

and 1 - X = 19.05%

With an 80.95% probability of scenario 1 and a 19.05% probability of scenario 2, the firm would be indifferent between short-term and long-term borrowing.

Proof:

	Outcome	Probability	Expected Value
Scenario 1	$3,600,000	.8095	$2,914,200
Scenario 2	5,700,000	.1905	1,085,850
	Total expected value		$4,000,050

The total expected value ($4,000,050) of short-term borrowing is virtually the same as the cost of long-term borrowing ($4,000,000). The slight difference is due to rounding.

9. Through hedging, the firm can reduce or eliminate the risk associated with rising interest rates. If interest rates do rise, the extra cost of borrowing money to actually finance the business can be offset by the profit on a futures contract.

Allison Boone, M.D. Case 9

Time Value of Money

Purpose: The case brings the time value of money into a legal settlement context, where present value concepts are frequently utilized. Many professors may also be able to draw on their own personal expertise to enhance the discussion of the case. The case deals with a high earning medical doctor and the loss to her family as a result of an accident.

Relation to the Text: The case should follow Chapter 9.

Complexity: The case is moderately complex and should require 1 hour.

Solutions

1. *Proposal Number One*
   $300,000 a year for the next 20 years

   $$PV_A = A \times PV_{IFA} \quad (n = 20, I = 6\%) \quad (Ap.D)$$

   $$PV_A = \$300,000 \times 11.470 = \$3,441,000$$

   Also

   $500,000 a year for the remaining 20 years

   Step 1
   $$PV_A = A \times PV_{IFA} \quad (n = 20, I = 6\%) \quad (Ap.D)$$

   $$PV_A = \$500,000 \times 11.470 = \$5,735,000$$

   Step 2

   $$PV = FV \times PV_{IF} \quad (n = 20, I = 6\%) \quad (Ap.B)$$

   $$PV = \$5,735,000 \times .312 = \$1,789,320$$

   Total present value

1st 20 years	$3,441,000
Remaining 20 years	1,789,320
Present value	$5,230,320

Proposal Number Two

Present value $5,000,000

Proposal Number Three

$50,000 a year for the next 40 years

$$PV_A = A \times PV_A \quad (n=40, I=6\%) \quad (Ap.D)$$

$$PV_A = \$50,000 \times 15.046 = \$752,3000$$

　　Also

$75 million at the end of 40 years

$$PV = FV \times PV_{IF} \quad (n=40, I=6\%) \quad (Ap.B)$$

$$PV = \$75,000,000 \times .097 = \$7,275,000$$

Total present value

40 year payment	$ 752,300
Payment at end of 40 years	7,275,000
Present value	$8,027,300

At a discount rate of 6 percent, proposal three has the highest net present value of $8,027,300.

2. Change the discount to 11 percent

   Proposal number one

   $300,000 a year for the next 20 years

   $PV_A = A \times PV_{IFA}$ (n = 20, I = 11%)   (Ap.D)

   $PV_A = \$300,000 \times 7.963 = \$2,388,900$

       Also

   $500,000 a year for the remaining 20 years

   Step 1

   $PV_A = A \times PV_{IFA}$ (n = 20, I = 11%)   (Ap.D)

   $PV_A = \$500,000 \times 7.963 = \$3,981,500$

   Step 2

   $PV = FV \times PV_{IF}$ (n = 20, I = 11%)   (Ap.B)

   $PV = \$3,981,500 \times .124 = \$493,706$

   Total present value

1 st 20 years	$2,388,900
Remaining 20 years	493,706
Present value	$2,882,606

Proposal Number Two

Present value $5,000,000

Proposal Number Three

$50,000 a year for the next 40 years

$$PV_A = A \times PV_{IFA} \quad (n = 40, I = 11\%) \quad (Ap.D)$$

$$PV_A = \$50,000 \times 8.951 = \$447,550$$

    Also

$75 million at the end of 40 years

$$PV = FV \times PV_{IF} \quad (n = 40, I = 11\%) \quad (Ap.B)$$

$$PV = \$75,000,000 \times .015 = \$1,125,000$$

Total present value

40 year payment	$ 447,550
Payment at end of 40 years	1,125,000
Present value	$1,572,550

At a discount rate of 11 percent, proposal two has the highest value of $5,000,000.

3. At a relatively high discount rate of 11 percent in question 2, the later payments lose much of their value. For example, the $75 million payment as part of proposal three only has a present value of $1,125,000 at a discount rate of 11 percent as compared to $7,275,000 at six percent. For this reason, the $5 million immediate payment in proposal two is the most favorable at the higher discount rate.

4. Punitive damages are added on to the economic damages. With the likelihood of $4 million in punitive damages, Sloan Whitaker may well want to take the case before a jury. However, we should keep in mind that offers for the out-of-court settlement have likely been influenced by the potential for punitive damages. Also, a jury verdict may be appealed and actual payment may be deferred many years into the future.

Because attorneys in cases such as this often get 1/3rd of the out-of-court settlement (or the jury determined value) as their fee, Sloan Whitaker is likely to consider this matter quite seriously. Of course, the final decision will rest with the Boone family, but Samuel Boone will be strongly influenced by the attorney's recommendation.

Although this question is not a financial one, it has financial implications for the student doing the case.

Billy Wilson—All American

Case 10

Time Value of Money

Purpose: The case provides the student with an interesting opportunity to examine the time value of money. Pro football contractual issues are frequently in the news so the student will be dealing with a contemporary situation. The student also will become familiar with deferred annuity payments.

Relation to Text: The case should follow Chapter 9.

Complexity: The case is moderately complex. It should require 1 hour.

Solutions

1. *Contract offer number one?*
    - Immediate signing bonus... $ 900,000
    - $850,000 at the end of each year for the next five years
      $PV_A = A \times PV_{IFA}$ (n = 4, i = 10%) (Ap.D)*
      $PV_A = \$850,000 \times 3.791 =$ 3,222,350
      Total present value $4,122,350
      *indicates appendix designation

    Contract offer number two
    - Immediate signing bonus... 200,000
      $100,000 at the end of each year for four years
      $PV_A = A \times PV_{IFA}$ (n = 4, i = 10%) (Ap.D)
      $PV_A = \$100,000 \times 3.170 =$ 317,000
    - $150,000 at the end of years five through 10)

      Step 1
      $PV_A = A \times PV_{IFA}$ (n = 6, i = 10%) (Ap.D)
      $PV_A = \$150,000 \times 4.355 = \$653,250$

      Step 2
      $PV = FV \times PV_{IF}$ (n = 4, i = 10%) (Ap.B)
      $PV = \$653,250 \times .683$.. 446,170
    - $1,000,000 a year at the end of years 11 through 40

      Step 1
      $PV_A = A \times PV_{IFA}$ (n = 30, i = 10%) (Ap.D)
      $PV_A = \$1,000,000 \times 9.427 = \$9,427,000$

      Step 2
      $PV = FV \times PV_{IF}$ (n = 10, i = 10%) (Ap.B)
      $PV = \$9,427,000 \times .386$... 3,638,822
      Total present value $4,601,992

    Contract offer number three
    - Immediate signing bonus... 1,000,000
    - $500,000 at the end of year one
      $PV = FV \times PV_{IF}$ (n = 1, i = 10%) (Ap.B)
      $PV = \$500,000 \times .909$ 454,5000
    - $1,000,000 at the end of year two
      $PV = FV \times PV_{IF}$ (n = 2, i = 10%) (Ap.B)
      $PV = \$1,000,000 \times .826$ 826,000
    - $1,500,000 at the end of year three
      $PV = FV \times PV_{IF}$ (n = 3, i = 10%) (Ap.B)
      $PV = \$1,500,000 \times .751$ 1,126,500

- $2,500,000 at the end of year four
  PV = FV x PV$_{IF}$ (n = 4, i = 10%) (Ap.B)
  PV = $2,500,000 x .683 1,707,500
- Bonus for Pro Bowl
  $200,000 x .25 = $50,000 expected value per year
  PV = A x PV$_{IFA}$ (n = 4, i = 10%) (Ap.D)
  PV$_A$ = $50,000 x $3.170 .... <u>158,500</u>
  Total present value... $5,273,000

2. *Contract offer by the Canadian football team*
   - Immediate signing bonus.. 1,100,000
   - $2,000,000 at the end of each year for three years
     x .80 probability the amount will be paid
     $1,600,000 expected value of the payment
     PV$_A$ = A x PV$_{IFA}$ (n = 3, i = 10%) (Ap.D)
     PV$_A$ = $160,000 x 2.487 .... <u>3,979,200</u>
     Total present value $5,079,200

3. The third contract proposal from the U.S. team ($5,273,000)

4. The second contract proposal from the U.S. team with the *late cash flows* would become much more attractive relative to the other contracts.

   Though the computation is not required, the value of the second contract proposal goes up to $7,388,055.

5. $5,273,000   Third contract proposal from the U.S. team
    <u>   x .90</u>
    $4,745,700   Remaining value after the agent's 10 percent fee
    <u>   x .67</u>
    $3,179,619   Aftertax value

6. They would put an even greater emphasis on early payments.

7. The value of an annuity:
   $$A = \frac{PV_A}{PV_{IFA}} \quad (n = 40, i = 10\%) \text{ (Ap.D)}$$

   $$A = \frac{\$5,273,000}{9.779} = \$539,217$$

8. Answers might include:
   - Possible extra revenues from commercials, personal appearances
   - The competition for his position on whatever team he signs a contract
   - Of course, many other answers also are possible.

Gilbert Enterprises　　　　　　　　　　　　　　　　　　　　　　　Case 11

Stock Valuation

Purpose: This case gives the student an opportunity to examine valuation concepts from both a theoretical dividend valuation model approach and a price-earnings ratio approach. Because an initial period of supernormal growth is assumed, a review of Appendix 10B is necessary for the case. However, this appendix is not difficult to follow. The case also makes strong use of ratios as part of the comparative P/E ratio analysis and should help the student better appreciate how ratios influence valuation.

Relation to Text: The case should follow Chapter 10.

Complexity: The overall case is moderately complex and should require 1 hour.

Solutions

1. There are two steps involved in using the valuation of a supernormal growth firm.
   A. Find the present value of supernormal dividends.
      $D_0 = \$1.20$
      $D_1 = \$1.20 \times 1.15 = \$1.38$
      $D_2 = \$1.38 \times 1.15 = \$1.59$
      $D_3 = \$1.59 \times 1.15 = \$1.83$

	Supernormal Dividends	Discount Rate $K_e = 10\%$	Present Value of Dividends During the Supernormal Period
D_1	$1.38	.909	$1.25
D_2	1.59	.826	1.31
D_3	1.83	.751	1.37
			$3.93

   B. Find the present value of the future stock price.
   $$P_3 = \frac{D_4}{K_e - G}$$

   $D_4 = D_3(1+g) \quad D_3 = 1.83, \; g = 6\%$

   $D_4 = \$1.83(1.06) = \$1.94$

   with $K_e = .10$

   $$P_3 \frac{\$1.94}{.10 - .06} = \frac{\$1.94}{.04} = \$48.50$$

   The present value of the future stock price is:

Stock Price after Three Years	Discount Rate 10%	Present Value of Future Stock Price
$48.50	.751	$36.42

   Adding together, the values found in Step 1 and Step 2, the valuation is $40.35.

Step 1	$ 3.93
Step 2	36.42
	$40.35

   Because the stock is only selling in the market for 35 1/4th, it appears to be undervalued.

2. Gilbert Enterprises has the second lowest P/E ratio of the four firms. Based on the financial information provided in Figure 1, this does not appear to be appropriate. First of all, Gilbert Enterprises has the fastest growth rate in earnings per share of any of the four firms. Furthermore, the growth is expected to accelerate to 15 percent over the next three years (as explained earlier in the case).

Gilbert Enterprises also has the second highest return on stockholder's equity. Only Reliance Parts has a higher return, but its return is achieved solely as a result of its high debt ratio of 68 percent. As we learned in Chapter 3, it is possible to generate a high return on equity using debt, but still have relatively low profitability. In fact, Reliance Parts has the lowest return on total assets of any firm in the industry.

In evaluating debt utilization as a separate item, Gilbert Enterprises once again looks attractive with a debt to total assets ratio of 33 percent. Only Standard Auto has a lower ratio.

We get further insight by evaluating market value to book value as well as market value to replacement value. In terms of market value to book value, Gilbert Enterprises appears to be overvalued relative to other firms in the industry. It's market value to book value ratio is 2.15 ($35.25 / $16.40). For the other three firms, the ratios are more conservative.

	Market Value	*Book Value*	*Market Value to Book Value*
Gilbert Enterprises	$35.25	$16.40	2.15
Reliance Parts	70.50	50.25	1.40
Standard Auto	24.25	19.50	1.24
Allied Motors	46.75	50.75	.92

But keep in mind that book value is a relatively meaningless concept because it is based on historical cost. A more meaningful analysis relates market value to replacement value. In this instance, we see that Gilbert Enterprises is the most conservatively valued of the four firms.

	Market Value	*Replacement Value*	*Market Value to Replacement Value*
Gilbert Enterprises	$35.25	$43.50	.81
Reliance Parts	70.50	68.75	1.03
Standard Auto	24.25	26.00	.93
Allied Motors	46.75	37.50	1.25

What about dividends? In terms of dividend yield, only Standard Auto provides a higher return to its stockholders.

In summarizing the variables under consideration, it appears that Gilbert Enterprises may be undervalued relative to its competitors. While it has the second lowest P/E ratio, it has the fastest growth rate in earnings per share, the highest return on assets, and the lowest ratio of market value to replacement value. The average P/E ratio for the four firms in the industry is 18.3. A strong case can be made that Gilbert Enterprises belongs at least at that level.

3. Since the answer to questions 1 and 2 indicate the firm may undervalued, Albert Roth should seriously consider recommending that the firm repurchase part of its shares in the marketplace.

There are two possible caveats. One is that the market tends to be efficient in the pricing of securities so that one could possibly argue that there is some missing information that justifies Gilbert Enterprises' relatively low valuation. While an extended discussion of this point goes beyond the scope of this case, it probably should be brought up.

Secondly, even if the stock is undervalued in the marketplace, the management of Gilbert Enterprises must make sure this is the best possible use of its funds. While the justification for a repurchase decision is not covered until Chapter 18 of the text, the instructor should at least make mention of the alternative uses of funds that must be considered in a stock repurchase decision.

Berkshire Instruments   Case 12

Cost of Capital

Purpose: The case gives the student additional opportunities to work with issues related to cost of capital. It focuses on the irrelevance of historical cost and the close relationship of retained earnings and new common stock in supplying equity capital. The concept of the *marginal* cost of capital is heavily stressed, and the use of the capital asset pricing model as an alternative to computing the cost of equity capital is also introduced.

Relation to Text: The case should follow Chapter 11.

Complexity: The case tends to be reasonably straightforward and requires about ½ hour.

Solutions

1. First determine the percentage composition in the capital structure.

	Dollar amount	Percentage composition
Bonds	$ 6,120,000	34
Preferred stock	1,080,000	6
Common equity	10,800,000	60
	$18,000,000	100

Then determine the aftertax cost of each component (for now assume common equity is in the form of retained earnings).

Cost of Debt

$$K_d = Y \text{ (Yield)} (1 - T)$$

$$\text{Approximate yield to maturity } (Y') = \frac{\text{Annual interest payment} + \frac{\text{Principle payment} - \text{Price of the bond}}{\text{Number of years to maturity}}}{.6 \text{ (Price of the bond)} + .4 \text{ (Principle payment)}}$$

$$Y' = \frac{\$93 + \frac{\$1,000 - \$890}{20}}{.6(\$890) + .4(\$1,000)}$$

$$= \frac{\$93 + \frac{\$110}{20}}{\$534 + \$400}$$

$$Y' = \frac{\$93 + \$5.50}{\$934} = \frac{\$98.50}{\$934} = 10.55\%$$

$$K_d = 10.55\% \, (.65)$$

$$K_d = 6.86\%$$

Cost of preferred stock

$$K_P = \frac{D_P}{D_P - F}$$

$$\frac{\$4.80}{\$60 - 2.60} = \frac{\$4.80}{\$57.40} = 8.36\%$$

*Cost of common equity
(retained earnings)*

$$k_e = \frac{D_1}{P_0} + g$$

D_1 = Earnings per share × .4 = \$3.00 × .4 = \$1.20

$P_0 = \$25$

g = the growth rate that will allow \$.82 to grow to \$1.20 over 4 years.

$$FV_{IF} = \frac{FV}{PV} = \frac{\$1.20}{\$.82} = 1.463$$

The growth rate is approximately 10%.

$$K_e = \frac{D_1}{P_0} + g = \frac{\$1.20}{\$25} + 10\% = 4.80\% + 10\% = 14.80\%$$

Now combine the weights and the costs.

		Cost (aftertax)	Weights	Weighted Cost
Bonds	K_d	6.86%	34%	2.33%
Preferred stock	K_P	8.36	6	.50
Common equity (retained earnings)	K_e	14.80	60	8.88
Weighted average cost of capital	K_a			11.71%

2. First compute the cost of new common stock.

$$K_n = \frac{D_1}{P_0 - F} + g$$

$$= \frac{\$1.20}{\$25 - \$2} + 10\% = 5.22\% + 10\% = 15.22\%$$

Then recompute the cost of capital.

		Cost (aftertax)	Weights	Weighted Cost
Bonds	K_d	6.86%	34%	2.33%
Preferred stock	K_P	8.36	6	.50
Common equity (new common stock)	K_n	15.22	60	9.13
Weighted average cost of capital	K_{mc}			11.96%

The size of the capital structure at which the cost of capital goes up is $7,500,000.

$$\frac{\text{Retained earnings}}{\text{Percent of common equity in the capital structure}} = \frac{\$4,500,000}{.60} = \$7,500,000$$

3. Based on the capital asset pricing model, the cost of common stock (required return) is 14.75 percent. This is quite close to the value derived using the dividend valuation model (K_e) in question 1 of 14.8 percent.

$K = R_f + ß (K_m - R_f)$
    $6\% + 1.25 (13\% - 6\%)$
    $6\% + 1.25 (7\%) = 6\% + 8.757 = 14.75\%$

Galaxy Systems, Inc.   Case 13

Divisional Cost of Capital

Purpose: The case combines risk analysis with discount rate considerations. To emphasize how many multidivisional corporations operate, the case actually gets into the topic of divisional hurdle rates. The student is able to see how different divisions in a corporation might have different required rates of return based on their risk exposure. In this particular case, a key risk measure for the consideration is beta. The student does not have to actually compute betas, only observe how they might be used. A simple definition of beta is also included in the case. Calculations related to net present value and internal rate of return are purposely simple to emphasize more conceptual items. Actually the IRRs can be found as exact values from Appendix D after only one calculation.

There also is additional emphasis on how financial decisions are made in a corporate culture.

Relation to Text: The case should follow Chapter 13. It also draws on material from many of the capital budgeting chapters.

Complexity: The overall case is moderately complex and should require 1 hour.

Solutions

1. *Proposal A*

    $$IRR = \frac{Investment}{Annuity}$$

    $$= \frac{\$2,355,600}{\$400,000} = 5.889 \qquad n = 10 \qquad \text{Appendix D}$$

    IRR = 11%

    NPV (10% discount rate for the auto airbags production division)
    Cost $2,355,600
    Present value of inflows = A x PV$_{IFA}$
    A = $400,000, n = 10, i = 10%   Appendix D
    Present value of inflows = $400,000 x 6.145 = $2,458,000

Present value of inflows	$2,458,000
Cost	2,355,600
Net present value	$ 102,400

    Proposal B

    $$IRR = \frac{\$2,441,700}{\$450,000} = 5.426 \qquad n = 10 \qquad \text{Appendix D}$$

    IRR = 13%

    NPV (15% discount rate for the aerospace division)
    Cost $2,441,700
    A = $450,000, n = 10, i = 15%
    Present value of inflows = $450,000 x 5.019 = $2,258,550

Present value of inflows	$2,258,550
Cost	2,441,700
Net present value	($ 183,150)

    Proposal C

    $$IRR = \frac{\$145,680}{\$15,000} = 9.172 \qquad n = 15 \qquad \text{Appendix D}$$

    IRR = 6%

    NPV (10% discount rate for the auto airbags production division)
    Cost $145,680
    A = $15,000, n = 15, i = 10%
    Present value of inflows = $15,000 x 7.606 = $114,090

Present value of inflows	$ 114,090
Cost	145,680
Net present value	($ 31,590)

Proposal D

$$IRR = \frac{\$1,262,100}{\$300,000} = 4.207 \qquad n = 8$$

Appendix D

IRR = 17%

NPV (15% discount rate for the aerospace division)
Cost $1,262,100
A = $300,000, n = 8, i = 15%
Present value of inflows = $300,000 x 4.487 = $1,346,100

Present value of inflows	$1,346,100
Cost	1,262,100
Net present value	$ 84,000

2. Proposal A should be accepted
    IRR > discount rate (11% > 10%)
    NPV is positive $102,400

   Proposal B should be rejected
    IRR < discount rate (13% < 15%)
    NPV is negative ($183,150)

   Proposal C should be rejected
    IRR < discount rate (6% < 10%)
    NPV is negative ($31,590)

   Proposal D should be accepted
    IRR > discount rate (17% > 15%)
    NPV is positive $84,000

3. While the decisions related to Proposals A and B appear to be straightforward, Proposals C and D require further discussion.

   Proposal C has a negative net present value and the internal rate of return of 6% is well below the required rate of return of 10%. Nevertheless, it calls for the development of special equipment to be used in the disposal of environmentally harmful waste material created in the manufacturing process. Given that the auto airbags production division is located in California, which has tough environmental laws, the project should probably be accepted. We are not told whether the installation is mandatory under the law, but there probably is adequate motivation to move forward with the project. Of course, if the installment of the equipment is required by law, then Galaxy must move forward regardless of the numbers.

   Proposal D has a positive net present value and the internal rate of return of 17 percent is well above the required rate of return of 15 percent for the division. However, the proposal appears to have even greater risk than projects normally undertaken in the aerospace division. While the high required rate of return for this division is supposed to cover the risk exposure of dealing in federal government contracts, Project D calls for the development of a microelectric control system for fighter jets that are still in the design stage. Even if the microelectric systems are successfully developed, there may not be a need for them if the other aerospace company cannot successfully develop fighter jets. Furthermore, the target market for the jets is in underdeveloped countries, which increases the uncertainty associated with this project. In the final analysis, top management might require an anticipated return of 20 percent or more to take on this highly speculative project.

4. The $300,000 that has already been spent on the initial research for Proposal B (radar surveillance equipment) is a sunk cost. The money has already been spent and should have no influence on subsequent decisions. Sometimes in the real world, egos get in the way of corporate decisions, and division heads (or other executives) push hard for the continuance of projects that they spent funds on to explore; but that is not justification to continue on. This is somewhat like buying stock in an underperforming company in the stock market. Sometimes, you just have to take your losses.

Of course, even if we considered the $300,000 that had already been spent, it would raise the total cost of the project and make it even less economical.

Further Overall Comments

Companies that use divisional required rates of return often do have difficulties in finding betas for firms that produce products comparable to a division. That is, finding a "pure play" comparison is difficult. Therefore, using the average beta for an entire industry may be the next best alternative. For example, if a division produces machine tools, its beta may be inferred from the entire machine tool industry rather than from a given firm in the industry.

Aerocomp, Inc. Case 14

Methods of Investment Evaluation

Purpose: The emphasis is on comparing the payback method, the internal rate of return, and the net present value approaches for a series of investments. As the student progresses through the calculations, the various advantages and disadvantages of the different approaches become evident. The reinvestment assumption of a high return project under the internal rate of return can be highlighted and evaluated. Capital rationing is also introduced into the case and plays a part in the analysis. Finally, the issue of reported earnings to stockholders versus sophisticated capital budgeting techniques is brought up and makes for interesting classroom discussion. Are stockholders more concerned with next quarter's earnings or long-term benefits?

Relation to Text: The case should follow Chapter 12. The internal rate of return calculations can be tedious and may be simplified by the use of calculators, such as the Hewlett-Packard 12C Model, described in Appendix E of the text, or other appropriate calculator models.

Complexity: The case is fairly straightforward. The computation of the internal rate of return can be time consuming if done by hand.

Solutions

1. Total Reported Earnings increases for each projects:

	Project A	Project B	Project C	Project D
Year 1:	$(13,250)	$ 29,313	$(60,000)	$ 192,206
Year 2:	$ (450)	$ 87,938	$(16,000)	$ 129,846
Year 3:	$ 25,494	$146,563	$ 61,640	$ (43,350)
Year 4:	$101,003	$234,500	$162,140	$ (62,475)
Year 5:	$ 63,315	$322,438	$262,640	$ (94,350)
Total:	$176,112	$820,752	$410,420	$ 121,877

   We are told in the case that Kay Marsh is sensitive to Aerocomp's level of earnings. Therefore, Project B, with over $820,000 in reported earnings increases (twice as much as any of the other projects), will be the one that attracts Kay's attention. (She may initially be swayed by the $192,206 that Project D brings in during the first year, but the losses in years three through five will probably cause her to reject that alternative quickly.)

   Note that Projects A and C both produce earnings decreases for the first two years. We would suspect that if Emily thinks that either of these two should be selected (on the basis of some other ranking method, such as NPV), she had better have some convincing arguments prepared!

2. Payback Period, IRR, and NPV of each alternative:

	Project A	Project B	Project C	Project D
Payback Period:	4 years	5 Years	5 Years	2 Years
IRR:	14.08%	7.18%	11.95%	12.48%
NPV @ 10%:	$39,971	($63,848)	$52,192	$20,609

   (Students may get slightly different values due to rounding.)

   Note: A few students may question the fact that Project B's cost has not been completely recovered in the five-year period shown, as the cost of the other projects has been. Therefore, they will claim, we are not using the proper time frame for our comparison of the projects. Of course, they are correct, and deserve extra points for their astute observation. In the case, Project B's amortization, or depreciation, was limited on purpose to highlight the effect of depreciation on reported income and cash flows.

3. a. According to the Payback Method, Project D should be selected. The initial investment of $510,000 is recovered in the second year.

   b. The chief disadvantage of the Payback Method is obvious at once: the method ignores cash flows occurring after the payback period. In this case such an omission is disastrous, since Project D's reported earnings and cash flows fall off significantly after the payback period and never recover. Another disadvantage of the Payback Method is that it does not consider the timing of cash flows during the payback period.

c. In general, the Payback Method should not be used. However, it is used from time to time because it is easy to understand, and because it favors projects which pay off quickly. This can be an important factor in some fast-paced industries where a quick return is important. The Payback Method may have some justification as a backup method, but not as the primary analytical tool.

4. a. According to the IRR method, Project A should be chosen. It returns nearly two percent more than the closest competing project.

b. Remember, that to achieve the IRR during a project's life, the project's cash inflows must be reinvested at the IRR rate. This may be difficult or impossible to accomplish when high IRR's are involved. (Suppose you were Aerocomp's financial manager, and you were getting the cash flows from Project A. What would you do with them: Pay dividends? Put them in a money market account at 7%—that was the going rate at that time? You might encounter a great deal of difficulty locating an investment that would pay you back the IRR rate of 14.08%.) As a matter of interest (no pun intended) if Project A's cash flows were reinvested at 7% annually instead of the IRR rate of 14.08%, the project's total return for the five-year period would drop to 11.84%.

c. Another disadvantage of the IRR method is that it does not give any consideration to project size. For example, the IRR method would select a project which returned $10 on a $1 investment over any of the projects in this case, even though the dollar return to the firm was only $9. This is not a problem when all projects with IRRs over the cost of capital can be selected, but when the projects are mutually exclusive, or when capital rationing is in effect (as it is in this case), the IRR method may lead the firm to make an incorrect choice.

(Note: It is important to avoid confusion on this point. The IRR and NPV methods will both accept and reject the same investments, but they will not give them the same ranking. In this case, projects A, C, and D are all acceptable per IRR and NPV. However, the IRR method would choose projects A, D, and C, in that order, while the NPV method would choose C, A, and D.)

d. If the size of Aerocomp's capital budget were not limited, the IRR method would accept projects A, C, and D. Project B, with an IRR of 7.18%, nearly three percentage points less than the cost of capital, would be rejected anyway.

5. a. According to the NPV method, Project C, with an NPV of over $52,000, will be chosen. It will add to the present value of the firm over $12,000 more than the next best project. Of course, under the IRR, Project A will be selected. Actually Project C is only a third place finisher under the IRR method.

b. If the size of Aerocomp's capital budget were not limited, the NPV method would accept projects A, C, and D. Project B, with an NPV of -$63,848, would be rejected anyway. Note that both the NPV and IRR methods rejected project B. This is because its return is less than the cost of capital.

c. The likely selection is Project C because of its high net present value. This is partly attributable to the fact that only one project can be selected. Had there not been capital limitations, one might put more emphasis on the IRR or use a profitability index approach. Of course, some instructors might select Project A as being preferable using other criteria, and that is fine. There may be some interesting opportunities for a classroom debate or discussion on these points.

Phelps Toy Company

Case 15

Capital Budgeting and Cash Flow

Purpose: The case gives the student a good opportunity to do cash flow analysis. The use of variable discount rates based on project risk gives insight into how some corporations adjust for risk exposure. Also, the use of an appropriate time horizon for analysis is highlighted. Some students may take a special interest in the case because of the discussion of the profitable world of baseball card collecting.

Relation to the Text: Though the case is closely related to Chapter 12, it should probably follow after Chapter 13 because of the risk dimensions in the discussion. Some instructors, however, may prefer to gloss over the latter and present the case after Chapter 12.

Complexity: The case is relatively straightforward and should require approximately 1 hour.

Solutions

1. First determine the expected value of the first year's sales.

Assumption	Sales	Probability	Expected Value
Pessimistic	$1,100,000	.25	$ 275,000
Normal	2,000,000	.40	800,000
Optimistic	3,750,000	.20	750,000
Highly optimistic	4,500,000	.15	675,000
		1.00	$2,500,000

Then project sales for the next 5 years.

Year 2	$2,500,000 x 1.20	=	$3,000,000
Year 3	3,000,000 x 1.20	=	3,600,000
Year 4	3,600,000 x 1.20	=	4,320,000
Year 5	4,320,000 x 1.10	=	4,752,000
Year 6	4,752,000 x 1.10	=	5,227,200

Then determine operating expenses and EBDT for the 6 years.

Year	Sales	Operating expenses (.70)	EBDT
Year 1	2,500,000	1,750,000	750,000
Year 2	3,000,000	2,100,000	900,000
Year 3	3,600,000	2,520,000	1,080,000
Year 4	4,320,000	3,024,000	1,296,000
Year 5	4,752,000	3,326,400	1,425,000
Year 6	5,227,200	3,659,040	1,568,160

Next determine the annual depreciation over the 6 years.

Year	Depreciation Base	Percentage Depreciation	Annual Depreciation
1	$2,800,000	.200	$560,000
2	2,800,000	.320	896,000
3	2,800,000	.192	537,600
4	2,800,000	.115	322,000
5	2,800,000	.115	322,000
6	2,800,000	.058	162,400

Then combine the data into a table similar to Table 12-11.

	Year 1	Year 2	Year 3	Year 4	Year 5	Year 6
EBDT	$750,000	$900,000	$1,080,000	$1,296,000	$1,425,600	$1,568,160
Depreciation	560,000	896,000	537,600	322,000	322,000	162,400
EBT	190,000	4,000	542,400	974,000	1,103,600	1,405,760
T (34%)	64,600	1,360	184,416	331,160	375,224	477,958
EAT	125,400	2,640	357,984	642,840	728,376	927,802
+ Depreciation	560,000	896,000	537,600	322,000	322,000	162,400
Cash flow	$685,400	$898,640	$ 895,584	$ 964,840	$1,050,376	$1,090,202

2. The discount rate will be based on the coefficient of variation of the first year's sales.

   The standard deviation was given as $1,226,000 and the expected value is $2,500,000.

   The coefficient of variation is:
   $$\frac{\$1,226,000}{2,500,000} = .4904$$

   Examining Figure 3 for a coefficient of variation of .4904, the discount rate should be 14 percent.

3. We next determine net present value.

Year	Cash flow (inflows)	Present Value Factor (14%)	Present Value
1	$ 685,400	.877	$ 601,096
2	898,640	.769	691,054
3	895,584	.675	604,519
4	964,840	.592	571,185
5	1,050,376	.519	545,145
6	1,090,202	.456	497,132
Present value of inflows			$3,510,131

Present value of inflows	3,510,131
Present value of outflows (cost)	2,800,000
Net present value	$ 710,131

   Based on the positive net present value of $710,131, the project appears to be feasible. The firm would be justified in going ahead with the investment.

4. A six year time horizon may be too short a time frame to fully assess the project. It assumes there will be no cash flow from the seventh year on. While many firms utilize a time frame of 5-10 years for conservative purposes, this may sometimes result in the rejection of a potentially profitable project that requires a longer time period for analysis. In this particular case, this was not a problem for the Phelps Toy Company as the project had a positive net present value over six years. Nevertheless, it could lead to an inappropriate decision for a long-life project in the future.

Inca, Inc. Case 16

Capital Budgeting with Risk

Purpose: The student goes through the statistical procedure of determining risk for investments. Though one investment alternative provides the higher net present value, is also has a much higher coefficient of variation and the student must take this into consideration in describing his or her results. The case is then expanded into six alternatives for which the student is asked to select the lowest risk option.

Relation to Text: This case should follow Chapter 13.

Complexity: This case is straightforward and should require 30-45 minutes to solve.

Solutions

1. Expected value of the net present value (standard)

Outcome	Probability	Expected Value
$1,050	.40	420
630	.40	252
(200)	.20	(40)
		632

$632,000

2. Expected value of the net present value (expanded)

Outcome	Probability	Expected Value
$2,812	.40	1,124.8
740	.40	296
(900)	.20	(180)
		1,240.8

$1,240,800

3. The expanded size restaurant alternative clearly has the higher net present value. ($1,240,800 vs. $632,000).

4. Standard Deviation = $\sqrt{\Sigma(D - \overline{D})^2 P}$

   D = outcome

   $\overline{D}$ = expected value

   P = probability

D	$\overline{D}$	$(D-\overline{D})$	$(D-\overline{D})^2$	P	$(D-\overline{D})^2 P$
1,050	632	418	174,724	.40	69,889.6
630	632	–2	4	.40	1.6
–200	632	–832	692,224	.20	138,444.8
					208,336.0

$\sqrt{208,336.0} = 456.4$

$456,400

5. Coefficient of variation (V) = $\dfrac{\text{expected value}}{\text{standard deviation}}$

	Standard size restaurant	Expanded restaurant
$\dfrac{\text{standard deviation}}{\text{expected value}}$	$\dfrac{\$456,400}{632,000} = .722$	$\dfrac{\$1,415,800}{1,20,800} = 1.141$

6. Based on the coefficient of variation, the standard size restaurant is much less risky (.722 versus 1.141).

   Earlier in question two, the preference was clearly for expanded size restaurants. The general principle is that you may not wish to always go with the highest return. Risk must be considered as well.

7. Coefficient of variation

4 standard, 1 expanded	$ 641,630 / 753,760 =	.851
3 standard, 2 expanded	832,460 / 875,420 =	.951
2 standard, 3 expanded	1,025,800 / 997,280 =	1.028
1 standard, 4 expected	1,220,400 / 1,119,040 =	1.091

   Based on the answer to question five as well as this question, the lowest-risk alternative is still the five standard restaurants with a coefficient of variation of .722.

Robert Boyle & Associates, Inc. Case 17

Going Public and Investment Banking

Purpose: The pros and cons of going public are considered in this case. Although the firm is a fictitious company, it is compared to a number of actual companies in the Real Estate Investment Trust (REIT) industry in order to establish the initial evaluation. The problem of capital shortage for the small private firm is the catalyst for considering the new offering. The potential dilution of new stock issues on earnings per share is carefully considered. In order to bring added interest to the case, there is a slightly nagging spouse who serves as a devil's advocate.

Relation to Text: This case should follow Chapter 15.

Complexity: The case is moderately complex and should require 1 hour.

Solutions

1. Computation of Robert Boyle & Associates P / E ratio:

			Industry P/E 14.0
Return on Equity:	*Boyle* 35.5%	*Industry* 12.8%	+.5
Return on assets:	*Boyle* 19.5%	*Industry* 8.7%	+.5
Debt to assets:	*Boyle* .45	*Industry* .31	–.5
Asset Turnover:	*Boyle* .30	*Industry* .22	+.5
Net Profit Margin:	*Boyle* 64.1%	*Industry* 37.5%	+.5
5-Yr EPS growth:	*Boyle* 9.7%	*Industry* 5.3%	+.5
		Net Additions and Subtractions:	+2.0
		Minus 1 to ensure a good sale:	–1.0
		Final P / E Ratio for Robert Boyle & Associates:	15.0

2. Total size of the stock issue necessary to yield $10 million in net proceeds:

    The size of the issue – the size times the spread percentage – out-of-pocket expenses = net proceeds

    X = the size of the issue
    $X - .065(X) - \$60,000 = \$10,000,000$
    $.935(X) = \$10,060,000$
    $X = \$10,759,358.29$,
    round to $10,800,000

3. Required rate of return on net proceeds: Let X = the amount of income necessary to be earned:

    (Old Net Income + X) / Total number of shares outstanding = old EPS
    ($4,100,000 + X) / 4,699,029* = $1.03
    $4,100,000 + X = $1.03 x 4,699.029
    $4,100,000 + X = $4,840,000
    X = $740,000

    ---
    *4,00,000 old shares + 699,029 new shares = 4,699,029
    Next compute the percent dollar return on the next proceeds.
    $740,000 / $10,800,000 = 6.85%

    Note that Robert Boyle & Associates earned a 19.5% return on assets in 1987, so we would expect that the company should have no problems producing an 6.85% return on the new assets to be obtained.

4. The total number of shares to be issued will be the two million from the existing stockholders plus the 699,029 originally planned. The decision by some of the existing stockholders to sell some of their shares makes no difference in this case—the company still needs to issue enough *new* shares to net $10,000,000. The two million shares from the existing stockholders are simply transferred from one set of people to another; the total number outstanding is not affected.

5. Summary of the advantages of going public:
   — Provides access to capital, which, in this case, appears difficult to obtain in any other way.
   — Provides a method by which the existing stockholders may liquidate their holdings to raise cash or to buy other securities (in order to diversify their portfolios).
   — Establishes a market value for the firm.

   Summary of the disadvantages:
   — Relatively high cost (over $700,000 in this case to raise $10 million).
   — Additional paperwork and reporting requirements.
   — Necessity to deal with the public (Mr. Boyle will spend more of his time in public relations).
   — Pressure for short-term results.
   — Possible loss of control of the firm if enough shares are issued, or if a hostile suitor attempts a takeover.

Conclusion: Robert Boyle & Associates is doing perfectly well as it is, and could conceivably continue doing so without getting involved in the new shopping center on Nantucket Island. However, the need to provide a market for the firm's shares and the need to provide a way for the existing stockholders to diversify their portfolios are strong arguments for going public (the shopping center development business is, after all, not without risk). Further, if the investors have any desire for growth, it appears they must go public to obtain the needed capital. From the limited information we have, the Nantucket Center project appears to be attractive. Therefore, it is probable that Robert Boyle and Associates will not be able to take the conservative approach—save up for years until they have enough to build it—because another firm will step in and build it themselves. All in all, it appears that the time for Robert Boyle & Associates to go public may have arrived.

Leland Industries

Case 18

Debt Financing

Purpose: The case gives the student a chance to understand the many factors influencing bonds. Initially the student concentrates on the variables affecting a bond rating and actually makes a basic bond rating decision. The relationship of bond ratings to yield to maturity also is stressed through various computations. The case also covers such innovative debt products as floating rate and zero-coupon rate bonds. Finally the use of hedging to cover interest rate exposure is explored.

Relation to Text: The case draws on material from Chapters 8, 10, 11 and primarily Chapter 16. It integrates cost of capital, hedging and long-term issues. The case should follow Chapter 16.

Complexity: The case is moderately complex. It should require 1-1½ hours.

Solutions

1. A potential bond issue by Leland would definitely not qualify for the AA1 rating that International Bakeries enjoys and would be well above the B3 rating of Savanah Products. The bond would undoubtedly fall somewhere between AA3 and A2.

   A comparative analysis with the three most similar firms is presented below.

	Dyer Pasteries	Gates Bakeries	Nolan Bread	Leland Industries
Rating	AA3	A1	A2	?
Debt to Total Assets	35%	42%	47%	44%
Times interest earned	6.0X	5.5X	4.9X	5.7X
Fixed charge coverage	3.6X	4.2X	3.8X	3.7X
Current ratio	2.8X	2.3X	2.1X	2.0X
Return on equity	19%	17.1%	15%	16.8%

   Leland generally falls below Dyer Pasteries on all measures except fixed charge coverage, so it is unlikely to qualify for an AA3 rating. The firm appears to fall between the A1 and A2 categories. Its debt ratio, times earned and return on equity ratios indicate it falls closer to the A1 category than the A2. However, its fixed charge coverage and current ratio are more in line with an A2 rating. On balance, A1 is probably the most appropriate answer.

2. The approximate yield to maturity (Y') formula is:

$$\frac{\text{Annual interest payment} + \dfrac{\text{Principle payment} - \text{Price of the bond}}{\text{Number of years to maturity}}}{0.6 \,(\text{Price of the bond}) + 0.4 \,(\text{Principle payment})}$$

International Bakeries

$$= \frac{\$103.50 + \dfrac{\$1{,}000 - \$1{,}100}{25}}{.6(\$1{,}100 + .4(\$1{,}000))}$$

$$= \frac{\$103.50 + \dfrac{-\$100}{25}}{\$660 + \$400}$$

$$= \frac{\$103.50 - \$4}{\$1{,}060} = \frac{\$99.50}{\$1{,}060} = 9.39\%$$

Gates Bakeries

$$= \frac{\$94.50 + \dfrac{\$1,000 - 920}{20}}{.6(\$920) + .4(\$1,000)}$$

$$= \frac{\$94.50 + \dfrac{\$80}{20}}{\$552 + \$400}$$

$$= \frac{\$94.50 + \$4}{\$952} = \frac{\$98.50}{\$952} = 10.35\%$$

Savanah Products

$$= \frac{\$157.50 + \dfrac{\$1,000 - \$1,150}{15}}{.6(\$1,150) + .4(\$1,000)}$$

$$= \frac{\$157.50 + \left(\dfrac{-\$150}{15}\right)}{\$690 + \$400}$$

$$= \frac{\$157.50 - \$10}{\$1,090} = \frac{\$147.50}{\$1,090} = 13.53\%$$

3. K_d (cost of debt) = Y (Yield) (1 – T)

International Bakeries	9.39% (1 – .35)	= 9.39% (.65)	= 6.10%
Gates Bakeries	10.35% (1 – .35)	= 10.35% (.65)	= 6.73%
Savanah Products	13.53% (1 – .35)	= 13.53% (.65)	= 8.79%

4. *Debt Outstanding*
   Year 1 $20,000,000 X .95 = $19,000,000
   Year 2 $19,000,000 X .95 = $18,050,000
   Year 3 $18,050,000 X .95 = $17,147,500

   Interest Payment on Debt
Debt outstanding	$17,147,500
Interest expense (10%)	1,714,750
Aftertax cost (1 – .35)	.65
Aftertax interest expense	$ 1,114,588

5. Interest savings on $20 million debt outstanding

Size of issue	$20 million
Interest savings (%)	1.25
Interest savings ($)	$250,000
Taxes (.35)	87,500
Aftertax benefit	$162,500

    Since the aftertax cost of hedging is $120,000, there is a net aftertax benefit of $42,500 per year

Aftertax interest savings	$162,500
Aftertax cost of hedging	120,000
Net aftertax benefit	$ 42,500

6. a) Present value of $1,000 zero-coupon rate bond.
    $PV = FV \times PV_{IF}$ (Appendix B)
    $FV = \$1,000, n = 20, i = 11\%$
    $PV = \$1,000 \times .124 = \$124$
    The bond price would be $124

    b) The number of bonds to be issued is:
    $$\frac{\$20,000,000}{\$124} = 161,290$$

    (note with $1,000 per value bonds, only 20,000 bonds would be issued)

    c) The danger is that the corporation is not paying any interest on an annual basis, and for this reason, the repayment obligation expands beyond the initial capital received. Thus, the firm must be sure that it is accumulating adequate funds to meet its future obligations (or will be able to issue new securities to refund the debt when it comes due).

Warner Motor Oil Company

Case 19

Bond Refunding

Purpose: The case gives the student a clear insight into the refunding process. The importance of the Call privilege is emphasized. Clearly, a refunding would not be feasible if the old issue had to be reacquired at market value. The case also provides an example of where a positive net present value may not be sufficient justification for taking action if the NPV is likely to be even larger in the future. There is also an optional question which allows the student to compare accounting implications with cash flow and net present value considerations. Normally, a refunding decision hurts accounting profits in the first year, and increases them in all subsequent years.

Relation to Text: The case draws primarily on material from Chapter 16. However, the student should be familiar with computing bond prices as presented in Chapter 10.

Complexity: The case is moderately complex. It should require 1 – 1½ hours.

Solutions

1. Price of Previously Issued Bonds

   Present value of interest payments
   $PV_A = A \times PV_{IFA}$ (n = 30, i = 5%)   Appendix D
   (A = 11.5%/2 × $1,000 = 5.75% × $1,000 × $57.50)
   PV_A = $57.50 × 15.372 = $883.89

   Present value of principal payment at maturity
   $PV = FV \times PV_{IF}$ (n = 30, i = 5%)   Appendix B
   PV = $1,000 × .231 = $231,000

   Total present value
   Present value of interest payments .... $ 883.89
   Present value of payment at maturity 231.00
   Total present value of price of the bond $1,114.89

2. Market price $1,114.89
   Par + 8% call premium 1,080.00
   Savings per $1,000 bond .... $ 34.89

   Added comment—On 30,000 bonds, this represents total savings of $1,046,700.

3. Refunding Analysis

   Outflows

   1. Payment of call premium
      $30,000,000 × 8% × $2,400,000
      $2,400,000 × (1 – .3) = $1,680,000

   2. Underwriting cost on new issue
      $30,000,000 × 2.8% = $840,000
      Amortization of cost ($840,000/15) (.3) $56,000 (.3) = $16,800 tax savings per year
      Actual expenditure $840,000
      PV of future tax savings $16,800 × 9.108* 153,014
      Net cost of underwriting expense on new issue $668,986

      *PV_{IFA} for n = 15, i = 7% (Appendix D)

   Inflows

   3. Cost savings in lower interest rates
      11.5% (interest on old bond)   × $30,000,000   = $3,450,000/year
      10.0% (interest on new bond)   × $30,000,000   =   3,000,000/year
      Savings per year $ 450,000
      Savings per year $450,000 × (1 – .3)   = $ 315,000 aftertax
      $ 315,000
      x   9.108 PV_{IFA} (n. = 15, i = 7%)   Appendix D
      $2,869,020   PV of A/T cost savings in interest rates

4. Underwriting cost on old issue
   Original amount $400,000
   Amount written off over 5 years at $20,000 per year 100,000
   Unamortized old underwriting cost.. $300,000
   Present value of deferred future write-off
   $20,000 × 9.108 (n = 15, i = 7%) 182,160
   Immediate gain in old underwriting cost write-off $117,840
   Tax rate x   .30
   Aftertax value of immediate gain in old underwriting cost write-off .... $ 35,352

Summary

	Outflows		Inflows
1.	$1,680,000	3.	$2,869,020
2.	668,986	4.	35,352
	$2,348,986		$2,904,372

PV of inflows $2,904,372
PV of outflows 2,348,986
Net of present value......... $ 555,386

The potential refunding has a positive net present value.

4. Gina and Al must consider whether interest rates will go even lower. If this is likely to be the case, they should wait to refund the old issue. It would be unwise to refund an issue, and then attempt to refund it again shortly thereafter if rates go down even further because of the large costs involved. Furthermore, if there is a deferred call provision on the new bonds issued after refunding, it may not be feasible to refund the new issue in any event.

5. With rates at 10.4 percent instead of 10 percent, the interest savings will be less.

We need to recompute the interest savings from step 3.

Cost savings in lower interest rates:

11.5% (interest on old bond)   × $30,000,000   = $3,450,000/year
10.4% (interest on new bond)   × $30,000,000   =   3,120,000/year
Savings per year $ 330,000
Savings per year   = $ 231,000 aftertax

$ 231,000
x   9.108   PV$_{IFA}$ (n. = 15, i = 7%)   Appendix D
$2,103,948   PV of A/T savings in interest rates

We now plug this figure into our summary of outflows and inflows. All prior values are the same.

Summary

	Outflows		Inflows
1.	$1,680,000	3.	$2,103,948
2.	668,986	4.	35,352
	$2,348,986		$2,139,300

PV of inflows....................	$2,139,300
PV of outflows.................	2,348,986
Net of present value.........	$ (209,686)

The potential refunding has a negative net present value and should not be undertaken.

6. The accounting numbers for 2001 are very different from net present value figures.

From an accounting viewpoint, the numbers for 2001 are as follows:

Payment of call premium..	−$2,400,000
Amortization of underwriting cost on new issue (annual)...	− 56,000
Interest savings	+ 450,000
Immediate write-off of unamortized underwriting cost on the old issue ($300,000) less the annual amortization of the annual amortization cost ($20,000) on the new issue.....................................	− 280,000
Before tax loss	−$2,286,000
Tax rate..	.30
Aftertax loss (Before tax loss x (1 – tax rate))	−$1,600,200

The large losses are due to the payment of the call premium and the write-off of unamortized underwriting costs on the old issue in 2001.

In 2002, the benefit of refunding begins to show up in terms of profitability.

Amortization of underwriting cost on new issue (annual)..	− $ 56,000
Interest savings	+ 450,000
Before tax profit	$394,000
Tax rate..	.30
Aftertax profit (Before tax profit x (1 – tax rate))	$275,800

Although the firm's profitability suffered in 2001 due to one time write-offs, the benefits begin in 2002 and take place for the remaining life of the new issue.

Midsouth Exploration Company

Case 20

Preferred Stock

Purpose: The case allows the student to examine many of the attributes of preferred stock. Particularly important is the cumulative feature when the company is in arrears, as well as a potential solution to that problem. The tax consequences of preferred stock to the corporate recipient is also considered. The case also provides a good opportunity to examine the comparative theoretical costs to the issuing corporation of preferred stock and common stock.

Relation to Text: The case draws on material from Chapters 11, 15, and 17. Because some material is related to dividends, the instructor may wait until after Chapter 18 to introduce the case (although such a delay is not really necessary).

Complexity: The case is moderately complex and should require 1 hour.

Solutions

1. No, payment of dividends on preferred stock is not a contractual obligation (as is the payment of interest on bonds). The only obligation is that the preferred stock dividends must be paid before common stock dividends.

2. The annual dividend is $8.50 per share and the firm is 2 ½ years behind on the payment.

   The answer is $21.25

Arrearage per share	$21.25
Shares outstanding	200.00
Total arrearage	$4,250,000

3.
Arrearage per share	$21.25
Premium	1.50%
Price per new share	$31.875

Share price	$31.875
Percent dividend	9.2%
Cash dividend	$2.9325

4. Aftertax preferred yield = Before-tax preferred stock yield [1 − (tax rate)(.30)]

   $$= 9.2\% \times [1 - (.35)(.30)]$$
   $$= 9.2\% \times (1 - .105)$$
   $$= 9.2\% \times .895$$
   $$= 8.234\%$$

5. Cost of preferred stock

$$k_p = \frac{D_p}{P_{p-F}} = \frac{\$2.9325}{\$31.875 - 0} = 9.2\% \text{ (this value was previously stipulated)}$$

Cost of new common stock

$$k_n = \frac{D_1}{P_{0-F}} + g = \frac{\$.50}{\$25 - \$1.20} = 9.75\%$$

$$\frac{\$.50}{\$23.80} + 9.75\% = 2.10 + 9.75\% = 11.85\%$$

There are no tax benefits to the issuing corporation for either security (as would be true of the payment of interest on debt).

6. Number of new shares of common stock:

$$\text{Number of new shares of common stock} = \frac{\text{Funds needed + out-of-pocket costs}}{\text{Net price to the corporation}}$$

$$= \frac{\$30,000,000 + \$250,000}{\$25 - \$1.20}$$

$$= \frac{\$30,250,000}{\$23.80} = 1,271,008 \text{ new shares}$$

Alpha Biogenetics Case 21

Poison Pill

Purpose: The case gives the student exposure to the poison pill and the entire issue of antitakeover amendments. Through running the numbers in the case, the student is able to view how poison pills can protect the current position of management. There is also dialogue in the case in which the virtues and drawbacks of poison pills are discussed. The student begins to get a feel for the issues of management entrenchment versus stockholder rights. Because there is also a venture capital investment and an IPO, the student is exposed to other areas of corporate finance as well.

Relation to Text: The case draws on material from Chapter 15 and Chapter 17. To a certain extent it goes beyond material in the text, but any new material is carefully explained within the context of the case.

Complexity: The case is moderately complex. It should require 1 – 1½ hours.

Solutions

1. Values for 2000

$$\text{Earnings per share} = \frac{\text{Earnings}}{\text{Shares}} = \frac{\$1,600,000}{5,000,000} = \$.32$$

$$\text{P/E} = \frac{\text{Stock price}}{\text{EPS}} = \frac{\$9.60}{\$.32} = 30$$

2.
Public price	$ 9.60
− Underwriting spread (5%)	.48
Net price	$ 9.12
x Shares (new shares sold)	2,000,000
Total proceeds	$18,240,000
− Out-of-pocket expense	120,000
Net proceeds	$18,120,000

3. Profit on sell of shares

Sales price	$ 9.60*
x Shares	1,200,000
Total proceeds	11,520,000
− purchase price	4,000,000
Profit	$ 7,520,000

*This assumes no underwriting spread on the secondary offerings of the venture capitalist shares. If the spread is included, the net sales price is $9.12 and the profit is $6,944,000. We are assuming the underwriter waives the spread.

$$\text{Rate of return} = \frac{\text{Profit}}{\text{Investment}} = \frac{\$7,520,000}{\$4,000,000} = 188\%$$

Given the risk that a venture capitalist takes in early stage financing, it is probably a reasonable return. Also, keep in mind that the venture capitalist had its funds tied up for a number of years to achieve the 188% total return.

4. Values for 2000

$$\text{Earnings per share} = \frac{\text{Earnings}}{\text{Shares}} = \frac{4,800,000}{5,000,000} = \$.96$$

$$\text{P/E} = \frac{\text{Stock price}}{\text{EPS}} = \frac{\$33.60}{\$.96} = 35$$

5.
Shares outstanding	5,000,000
x Percent ownership	25%
Number of Shares	1,250,000
x Price per share	$33.60
Total cost	$42,000,000

6. The inside control group owns 1.8 million shares.
   An unfriendly, outside party could acquire the remaining 3.2 million shares out of the 5 million shares outstanding.

   In order to maintain their majority position, the inside control group would need to buy 1,400,001 shares. This would give them a total of 3,200,001 shares.

Old shares	1,800,000
New shares	1,400,001
	3,200,001

   This represents one more share than the unfriendly, outside party owns.
   The total dollar cost would be:

Stock price	$33.60
x Percent of price at which shares may be purchased	70%
Net stock price	$23.52
x Number of shares	1,400,001
Total cost	$32,928,023

7. In many cases, it appears that poison pills are intended to provide management with job security rather than maximize stockholder wealth. In fact, research indicates that poison pill announcements are often met with a slightly negative response in the stock market.

   Of course, the counter argument is that poison pills allow management to take a long-term perspective without fear of being ousted and also puts the firm in a strong bargaining position in the event of a potential tender offer.

   Although there is no one correct answer to this question and either side of the issue can be justified, most large institutional investors do not like poison pill provisions.

Montgomery Corporation

Case 22

Dividend Policy

Purpose: The key issue is whether the firm's cash dividend should be considered an active or residual variable in setting the actual payment. There is enough bickering between directors and officers of the firm to give the student plenty of insight into this issue. Though Montgomery Corporation is a fictitious firm in the retail industry, the student is given enough information to compare its dividend policy to Dillard's, J.C. Penney, Wal-Mart, and others. The student is also asked to use the dividend valuation model, to consider capital structure issues, and also evaluate the suitability of a stock dividend versus a cash dividend.

Relation to Text: The case should follow Chapter 18. It is also assumed that the student is familiar with capital structure considerations (Chapter 11) and common stock (Chapter 17).

Complexity: The case is moderately complex. It should require 1 hour.

Solutions

1. a. From Figure 1, we note that Dividends per Share for the years 1981-1987 were:

1981	1982	1983	1984	1985	1986	1987
$1.36	$1.36	$1.48	$1.70	$1.76	$1.76	$1.96

    The firm is following a constant dividend policy with increases as the company grows. Note that the total amount committed to common dividends has increased each year, but it's the dividend per share figure that counts. Given the increasing number of shares outstanding each year, the directors have been sure that DPS has remained constant or increased slightly on an annual basis.

    b. In Figure 2, we see that all of Montgomery's competitors are either following the same policy that Montgomery is, or they are striving to increase the dividend every year. Dollar General held to a $.20 dividend in 1986 even though EPS decreased over 75%! In 1985 Dollar General actually increased the dividend by over 17% in spite of a 14% decrease in EPS. Clearly, dividend stability and growth is perceived as important in the retailing industry. Even Wal-Mart, a growing company which might be expected to emphasize capital growth over dividends, follows the general trend. (It is interesting to note that Montgomery generally has the highest average payout ratio in the industry. That's to be expected of an old firm that has been paying and increasing dividends for many years.)

2. a. Given that $D_1 = \$2.10$, $g = 7.1\%$, and $P_0 = \$35$, K_e, the expected return to the common stockholder is:

    $$K_e = \frac{\$2.10}{\$35} + 7.1\%$$

    $$= 6\% + 7.1\%$$

    $$= 13.1\%$$

    b. If Don's proposal is adopted, and next year's dividend is zero, but g rises to 14%, the expected return to the stockholders is:

    $$K_e = \frac{0}{\$35} + 14\%$$

    $$= 0 + 14\%$$

    $$= 14\%$$

    It appears that if Montgomery adopted Don's suggestion, the stockholders would realize a 0.9% increase in their expected return. By this calculation alone, then, we might conclude that Don's idea is a good one; the firm should adopt a residual dividend policy. However, note that the stockholders would only realize Don's 14% gain if they sell their shares, while the firm's current dividend policy gives the stockholders 13.1%. Given that situation, and the fact that the 1986 Tax Reform Act and subsequent legislation eliminated almost all the advantages of a capital gain at the time of this case, one might well argue that the stockholders are better off under the current policy. Further, note that the stockholders only appear to be better off under the new policy if g does, in fact, rise to 14%, which is speculative at best. If g turns out to be less than 13.1%, for example, the old policy will appear to be superior. It is reasonable to assume that if the dividend is retained and invested, g will increase, and intuitively we believe it should increase sufficiently to produce a total return greater than before, but there is no hard evidence that it will do so.

3. Don's argument rests on the principle that the capital budget, as well as the dividend, must be paid for solely out of net income for the current year, and, of course, this is not so. It is the amount of cash available that is the limiting factor. Referring to Figure 1, we see that Montgomery's cash balance for 1987 is $3,235 million, so that is the maximum size that the capital budget plus dividend payment can be without selling off assets or seeking outside financing. (This is an important point.) We often speak of financing the capital budget, or indeed, paying dividends, out of retained earnings. We tend to speak of retained earnings as if they were cash. They are not, of course; only claims on assets, of which cash is but one. If retained earnings were to be entirely used up in financing the capital budget, then some of the firm's assets would have to be sold in the process.

4. a. The cost of internal equity financing is, of course, 13.1%, which was computed in question 2a, above. The cost of external equity financing would be slightly higher due to flotation costs.
   b. Given that the firm can sell bonds priced to yield 13%, the aftertax cost of debt is 13% x (1 − .25) = 9.75%.
   c. This might throw the debt-equity mix out of proportion. Excessive use of debt might not only increase the cost of debt financing, but all other sources of financing as well.

5. Mr. Autry's comments strike at the heart of the residual dividend policy. That policy presumes that the stockholders have no preferences about the form of repayment they receive from their investment—only that the highest possible return be achieved. If, on the other hand, the stockholders do have a preference, then the residual policy may not be the best. There is no hard and fast rule on establishing whether or not the stockholders have a preference, or how strong it might be. Strong cases can be argued for either point of view and the subject remains controversial. It does appear from a study of Figure 2 that the managers of firms in the retailing business do believe that their stockholders have a preference, and that preference is for current income in the form of dividends.

6. The firm could pay a stock dividend in place of the cash dividend, and some stockholders might be satisfied with that. However, the majority would probably recognize that they had not received anything at all. A stock dividend is merely a paper entry creating more shares. It would only be perceived as beneficial if total stockholders' cash dividends increased as a result. (This, of course, would defeat the proposed purpose of the stock dividend—to conserve funds.)

7. As we mentioned in question 5, there is no universal agreement on this question. Some would argue that dividends do not matter and some would argue that they do. Most would agree, however, that if the firm does pay taxes, and if there are flotation costs associated with outside equity financing, and if there are costs associated with bankruptcy, then capital structure does matter, and dividend policy matters. Intuitively, and in the face of the obvious custom in the retailing industry, we would view a decision by a mature firm such as Montgomery to go to a residual dividend policy with some misgivings. Such a policy is perhaps best left to a younger firm.

Orbit Chemical Company

Case 23

Dividend Policy

Purpose: This case has a completely different emphasis from the prior dividend case, Montgomery Corporation. The Orbit Chemical Company case stresses the critical emphasis of the statement of cash flows in determining whether a company has the ability to make dividend payments. The emphasis is away from the relation of earnings to dividends, and toward the importance of cash flow. It truly forces the student to do insightful financial analysis as the answer to question one is not obvious. Some instructors may want to give clues to help the students. There is also an interesting side issue related to the repurchase of shares in the open market, and the associated impact on earnings per share and stock price. Executive stock options are also included in the analysis.

Relation to Text: This case should follow Chapter 18.

Complexity: The case is moderately complex. It should require 45 minutes.

Solutions

1. If the student properly assess the financial statements, he or she will see there is no need to reduce the cash dividend.

    The dividend payout ratio is relatively high at 61.3% ($.65 dividends per share/$1.06 earnings per share). However, this presents no real cause for concern. Furthermore, the firm only has $35 million in cash and marketable securities at year-end 2000, but that also should not be a problem.

    The real key to the analysis can be found in Figure 3, the statement of cash flows. Here, we see the firm had $181 million in net cash flows from operating activities. More specifically, net income plus depreciation was equal to $166 million. This was available to cover cash dividends of $65 million and increases in plant and equipment of $50 million.

Net income plus depreciation	$166 million
– Cash dividends	65 million
– Increase in plant and equipment	50 million
Excess funds	$ 51 million

    The firm could not only cover the dividends, but use the excess funds (a term roughly the equivalent to free cash flow) to almost double the dividend.

    The problem was that Robert Osborne had used these funds and part of a high beginning cash balance to reduce $120 million of long-term debt that was not due until 2016 (see financing activities under statement of cash flows). This action was probably ill advised and hopefully a one time occurrence. The firm's total debt to total assets ratio was down to 42.5 percent ($370 million/$870 million) by year-end 2000. Even if the $120 million portion of debt due in 2016 had not been paid off, and $120 million was added to the numerator and denominator of the above ratio, the total debt to total assets ratio would have still been a relatively healthy 49.5% ($490 million/$990 million) at year-end 2000. With $500 million in equity, total debt would have still been less than equity and long-term debt considerably less.

    The firm clearly generates enough cash flow to meet its dividend obligations. This should be a higher priority for the firm than partially retiring debt that is not due for 16 years.

    The true capability of a firm to pay its dividends can normally be found in the operating activities section of the statement of cash flows and not in the income statement or balance sheet.

2. To determine the number of shares that can be repurchased with $30 million, you first must determine the market price of the stock.

Earnings per share	$1.06
Price-earnings ratio	7
Stock price	$7.42

    By dividing $30 million by $7.42, we see that 4,043,127 shares can be repurchased.

3. The earnings are $106,000,000
   The shares outstanding are 100,000,000 − 4,043,127 = 95,956,873

   $$\text{Recomputed earnings per share are}: \frac{\text{Earnings}}{\text{Shares}} = \frac{\$106,000,000}{95,956,873} = \$1.10$$

4. Earnings per share $1.10
   Price-earnings ratio .... x 10
   Stock price $11.00

5. Stock price $11.00
   Option price 5.00
   Profit per share $6.00
   Shares .... x 50,000
   Total before tax profit $300,000

6. The stock market's reaction is quite likely to be negative to Robert Osborne exercising his options. By using 50,000 of his options to buy and resell stock now, he is indicating that he thinks $11.00 might represent the current upside potential for the stock for now. Actually investors are getting mixed signals. One is positive in that Orbit Chemical Company repurchased over four million of their own shares; the other is negative in that the CEO is selling ¼th of his shares covered by stock options.

   The insightful investor might ask further questions such as, "Does Robert Osborne have a particular need to exercise ¼th of his stock options now?" If he is using the profits to pay off personal debt, that might be acceptable. If her merely thinks this is a good time to take a profit, it would not be acceptable to other investors.

Hamilton Products Case 24

Convertibles

Purpose: The case encourages the student to more fully appreciate the financial characteristics of convertible bonds. It also allows the student to see that the pure bond value is not necessarily stable, but may change because of changing interest rates or business risk. The student not only views upside potential, but increasing downside exposure as well.

Relation to Text: The case should follow Chapter 19. However, the student will also need to utilize material from Chapter 10 for a bond value computation.

Complexity: The case tends to be reasonably straightforward and requires about ½ hour.

Solutions

1. Conversion value = conversion ratio x common stock price
   $884.25 = 27 x $32.75
   Conversion premium = convertible bond price – conversion value
   $115.75 = $1,000.00 – $884.25

2. First determine the conversion value:
   Conversion value = conversion ratio x common stock price
   $1,228.50 = 27 x $42.50
   Then determine the conversion premium:
   Conversion premium = convertible bond price – conversion value
   $21.50 = $1,250.00 – $1,228.50

3. First determine the conversion value:
   Conversion value = conversion ratio x common stock
   $803.25 = 27 x $29.75
   Then determine the price of the convertible bond:
   Convertible bond price = conversion value + conversion premium
   $901.25 = $803.25 + $98

4. Pure Bond Value
   Present value of interest payments
   $PV_A = A \times PV_{IFA}$ (n = 17, i = 10%)
   PV_A = $65 x 8.022 = $521.43
   Present value of principal payment (par value) at maturity
   $PV = FV \times PV_{IF}$ (n = 17, i = 10%)
   PV = $1,000 x .198 = $198.00

Present value of interest payments	$521.43
Present value of principal payment at maturity	198.00
Total present value or pure bond price	$719.43

5. Andre should probably not take too much comfort in the pure bond price. The convertible bond is selling for $901.25 as indicated in question 3 and the pure bond value is $719.43. That indicates a potential loss of $181.82 or 20.2 percent ($181.81/$901.25). Furthermore, there is always the danger of interest rates on comparable bonds going even higher. Originally, the pure bond value was $853.17, which certainly would have provided more comfort.

Security Software, Inc.   Case 25

Convertibles

Purpose: The case allows the student to view the hybrid nature of convertible securities. While it would be very difficult for the firm to issue either equity or bonds in the post-recession bear market of mid-2002, convertible securities offer the opportunity to enter the market at a lower interest rate and at a higher conversion price than the stock price the firm currently has. However, the case also illustrates the potentially downward effect of convertibles on earnings per share. An interesting feature of the case is that it traces stock price declines during the Internet bust.

Relation to Text: The case should follow Chapter 19.

Complexity: The case is moderately complex. It should require 1 to 1½ hours.

Solutions

1. a. $30   Million.................... Par value
       7.5% .... Interest rate
       $2.25 Million.................... Interest

   b. $30 million total issue / $1,000 par value = 30,000 bonds
      30,000 bonds x 40 conversion ratio = 1,200,000 potential new shares of common stock.

2. $30 million total issue / $19.50 stock price = 1,538,462 new shares

3. $30 million total issue / $35 stock price = 857,143 new shares
   This is not very realistic. First of all, there is no assurance the stock price will get up to $35 from its current level of $19.50. Secondly, SSI needs the $30 million now to remain competitive so it is unlikely the firm can wait until the stock price gets up to the $35.

4. $30   Million............ Total issue
       3.5%   .... Interest savings
   $1,050,000 .... Annual interest savings

5. With a conversion ratio of 40, the bonds will go up to a value of at least $1,400 (40 x $35). A conversion premium may call for even a slightly higher value.
   The bondholders do not need to convert immediately. They can merely ride the price of the bond up with the common stock.

6. The corporation could force a conversion through calling in the bonds at close to par when they are trading well in excess of par. In order to avoid the call at close to par, the bondholders would convert to common stock at the stock's advanced value (perhaps 40 shares at $35 or $1,400.)
   Also, a step-up in the conversion price after a specified period of time would tend to force bondholders to convert. If the conversion price went from $25 to $30, the conversion ratio would decline from 40 to 33.33 ($1,000 per value / $30 conversion price = $33.33 conversion ratio). The bondholder would have a strong incentive to convert before the step-up in the conversion price and the accompanying reduction in the conversion ratio. This assumes that the actual price of the common stock in the market has gone up enough to make a conversion desirable.

7. a. Earnings before interest and taxes $15,000,000
       Interest ($1,000,000 from the table in Question 7 plus $2,225,000 from the
         answer to Question 1 3,225,000
       Earnings before taxes $11,775,000
       Taxes (30%) 3,532,500
       Earnings after taxes .... $ 8,242,500

   $$\text{Basic earnings per share} = \frac{\text{Earnings after taxes}}{\text{Shares of common stock}} = \frac{\$8,242,500}{1,000,000} = \$.824$$

b. Diluted earnings per share = $\dfrac{\$8,242,500 + \$1,575,000^*}{1,000,000 + 1,200,000} = \dfrac{\$9,817,500}{2,200,000} = \$.446$

$$\begin{array}{rl} * & \$2,250,000 \quad \text{(Question 1)} \\ & \underline{.70} \quad (1-\text{tax rate or } 1-.30) \\ & \$1,575,000 \end{array}$$

8. The convertibles increase basic earnings per share by slightly over $.12 from $.70 to $8.24. However, diluted earnings per share are down by over $.25 from the initial value of $.70 to $.446. The need to show diluted earnings per share is a serious drawback to convertibles. Security analysts will be provided with both basic EPS and diluted EPS, but they tend to put more emphasis on the latter.

Optional Comment by Instructor

SSI may want to reduce the size of the deal or redesign the deal so that it will be less dilutive. One possibility would be to slightly raise the interest rate but increase the conversion price (and thus reduce the conversion ratio). Sensitivity analysis could be employed here.

National Brands vs. A-1 Holdings

Case 26

Merger Analysis

Purpose: This case features a surprise attack tender offer. The acquisition candidate decides to counter with a Pac Man defense in which they make an offer for the potential acquiring company. Both firms are considering various financing packages to establish their strategy including heavy leverage and the use of acquired assets as collateral. The student must consider the feasibility of the plans as well as the impact on stockholder wealth maximization. The student is also asked to consider social responsibility (good guy versus bad guy) issues related to the merger.

Relation to Text: The case should follow Chapter 20. Because the case covers many important questions in corporate finance, it may be used as an integrating exercise for many of the prior chapters.

Complexity: The case is somewhat complex. It is likely to require 2 hours.

Solutions

1. a. According to Figure 1, there are 113,640,000 shares of National Brands outstanding. But, A-1 already owns 5% of them, or 5,682,000, so it will only have to buy the remaining 107,958,000. At $55 each, the total price will be $5,937,690,000 (a little over $5.9 billion).

   b. The amount of liquid assets (i.e., cash and equivalents) on hand at National is $1,153,000,000. If A-1 can use this amount to offset the amount of borrowing required, the total amount it will have to borrow is
   $5,937,690,000 − $1,153,000,000 = $4,784,690,000

   c. After the purchase, A-1's total debt will consist of:

A-1's old debt:	$1,899,500,000
National's debt:	$2,110,300,000
Amount borrowed:	$4,784,690,000
Total:	$8,794,490,000

   Since all the funds to make the purchase were borrowed, A-1's total equity remains $395,000,000 after the purchase. Its debt to equity ratio after the purchase, therefore, is:
   $8,794,490,000 / $395,000,000 = 22.26 to 1!

   This is astonishing. Such high debt to equity ratios are not normally encountered except in financial institutions, such as banks. (In fact, A-1's balance sheet resembles that of a bank—over 75% of its assets are in cash and equivalents, lending credence to the charge that corporations such as A-1 aren't "real" corporations after all, merely shells, or deposit accounts used by their owners to make acquisitions.)

   Given such a high debt to equity ratio, it is difficult to imagine how Mr. O'Brien could finance the purchase of National using debt sources.

   d. In *b*, above, we computed that $4,784,690,000 was needed to make the purchase. If A-1 issues stock at $13 a share to raise the funds, it will need to issue 368,053,077 new shares.

   e. The total number of shares outstanding at A-1 after the purchase will be the 61,800,000 old shares plus 368,053,077 newly issued ones. Total expected earnings are the $152,000,000 A-1 originally expected plus $400,000,000 from National. So, A-1's EPS after the purchase will be:

   ($152,000,000 + $400,000,000) / ($61,800.00 + $368,053,077)
   = 552,000,000 / 429,853,077) = $1.28

   f. $1.28 represents a 48% decline from A-1's previous expected EPS of $2.46 (the decline, of course, was caused by the fact that National's P/E is much higher than A-1's). A-1's stockholders will not be pleased, unless Mr. O'Brien can convince them that they will be better off in the long run (unlikely—National's growth rate is not high enough), or he has some other plan in mind, such as selling off pieces of National at a profit. National's stockholders, on the other hand, will realize an immediate 15% capital gain. ($7.12 / $47.88) = 15 percent. They may be more satisfied, though 15 percent is a relatively small premium.

2. a. Employing the Pac Man defense will cost National $17 a share times the 61,800,000 shares of A-1 outstanding, or $1,050,600,000.

   b. A-1 has $1,736,800 of liquid assets available. Using this amount to offset the amount of National stock to be issued brings the total amount of cash needed to be raised down to:
   $1,050,600,000 − $1,736,800,000 = −$686,200,000

   It's a rather surprising result that National could buy A-1 without spending any of its own money at all! The Cash and Equivalents balance on hand at A-1 is more than enough to cover the cost of the company. Of course, National will have to assume all of A-1's debt too, which is rather substantial. See the next answer, below.

   c. National's total debt after the purchase will be its old debt plus A-1's debt:

National's old debt:	$2,110,300,000
A-1's old debt:	$1,899,500,000
National's new debt:	$4,009,800,000

   National's total equity after the purchase will simply be its old equity, $3,050,000,000. Therefore, National's debt to equity ratio after the purchase will be:
   $4,009,800,000 / $3,050,000,000 = 1.31 to 1

   The new ratio of 1.31 to 1 is nearly double National's old ratio of .69 to 1, so the company will probably want to use at least some of A-1's cash to reduce its debt load instead.

   This situation illustrates why companies with large cash balances (and small debt balances) are attractive takeover targets.

   d. If National uses A-1's $1,736,800,000 cash and equivalents balance to pay down A-1's $1,899,500,000 debt balance, it will not have any left to apply to the stock issue. Therefore National will have to issue enough of its own shares at $47.88 each to cover A-1's entire cost of $1,050,600,000:
   $1,050,600,000 / $47.88 = 21,942,356 shares

   e. The total number of shares outstanding at National after the purchase will be the 113,640,000 old shares plus 21,942,356 newly issued ones. Total expected earnings are the $400,000,000 National originally expected plus $152,000,000 from A-1. So National's EPS after the purchase will be:
   ($400,000,000 + $152,000,000) / (113,640,000 + 21,942,356)
   = $552,000,000 / 135,582,356 = $4.07

   f. Yes, Mr. Hall is correct. The purchase of A-1 will not dilute National's earnings, at least in the coming year. They actually increase from $3.52 to $4.07.

3. If National's P/E remains at its previous value of 13.6, its stock price can be expected to rise to $4.07 x 13.6 = $55.35. Of course, it is highly unlikely that its P/E will remain at its previous value. A-1's old P/E was only 5.3, less than half that of National. It is likely, therefore, that investors will lower their expectations for National somewhat, despite its higher earnings. If National's P/E drops only as far as 11.76, its stock price will remain at $47.88.

Note—students may question why A-1 has a higher growth rate than National, yet its P/E is much lower. The answer lies in the fact that the P/E ratio does not depend on investors' growth expectations alone. In this case the P/E is inhibited by A-1's extremely high debt ratio.

4. a. As a result of A-1's offer to buy National, National's stockholders stand to realize a 15% capital gain, but National's management is against the move and will try to convince the stockholders to reject it. On the other hand, A-1's stockholders stand to realize a 31% capital gain ($13 to $17) if National buys A-1, and nothing in the case indicates that Mr. Kelly O'Brien would resist such a deal. Therefore, it seems likely that National's bid to purchase A-1 will prevail. It is tough to dismiss the suggestion that he may have engineered the entire situation merely to elicit the Pac Man response from National. In fact, this suggestion was reported in the press concerning the companies upon which this case is based.

b. It is difficult to say whether or not National's stockholders are better off as a result of their company's employment of the Pac Man defense. On the one hand they have been denied the chance for a 15% capital gain. On the other, they have gained a set of assets which may or may not achieve an equal gain, even in the long term. Further, the assets were not purchased as a part of an integrated capital budgeting program, but were obtained under duress. On balance, it would appear that A-1's stockholders would be the big winners in this situation.

c. Those who take sides with the corporate "raiders" would say that they provide a valuable function in the economy—weeding out inefficiency. They do this by buying inefficiently managed companies and restructuring them into more effective units. In the long run, they say, the economy as a whole is strengthened. Opponents charge that the practice is unfair to employees who are uprooted and often lose their jobs in the restructurings, and they maintain that business ought to concentrate on making money by producing quality products rather than making it by trading companies. In the long run, they say, the economy as a whole is weakened. The issue goes far beyond a case in finance, essentially becoming one of ethics and point of view. The truth is probably a blend of the two views, or the classic "it depends." At the very least we can probably say that such decisions should not be made purely on the basis of the financial aspects of the situation.

KFC and the Colonel   Case 27

General Business Considerations

Purpose: This case is different from the prior 22 and may only appeal to certain instructors. It is a real-world documentation of the process that Colonel Harland Sanders went through in selling out Kentucky Fried Chicken to John Young Brown, Jr. in 1964. It is really part management and part finance. The student also views the early trials and tribulations of the Colonel as well as the enormous success of his company after he sold it for the very modest price of $2 million. The student is asked to consider whether the Colonel acted prudently in accepting the offer based on the information he had at the time and what additional steps he might have taken in the negotiations.

Relation to Text: The case can be introduced at any point as interesting reading, but should probably follow the material on long-term financing and mergers.

Complexity: The case involves the absorption of information rather than complex analysis and should probably require 45 minutes.

Solutions

A number of issues can be raised concerning Sanders' approach in connection with the sale to Brown and Massey.

First of all, it would appear that he should have consulted with more than one individual (Harman) before he made a proposal to sell at $2,000,000. He should have discussed the matter with Claudia, who had been his business partner and later his wife before coming to a final decision. As a matter of courtesy, he should also have advised his office staff that he was considering the sale and perhaps asked for their advice. Most important, he should have reviewed the proposed sale with a CPA firm and with an attorney familiar with this type of transactions. Although Brown served earlier as Sanders' attorney, Brown was now on the other side of the fence, representing his own interests. Finally, when Sanders did decide to consult with Harman, he should have gone to discuss the matter with him alone—not with Brown and Massey. While there is no reason to suspect that Harman may have acted improperly, it is still apparent that as the largest franchisee at the time, his advice to Sanders may not have been made from a disinterested point of view.

What are some of the other options that Sanders may have considered other than the $2,000,000 cash price?

Initially, $2,000,000 "cash" turned out not to be exactly $2,000,000 as of the date of the sale since the balance of $1,500,000 was to paid over five years after the down payment of $500,000. It was, therefore, a discounted "$2,000,000." Was there a provision in the agreement to compensate Sanders for the use of capital during the five-year period? Also, was there some guarantee—perhaps on the part of Massey, the "Nashville millionaire"—to make sure that Sanders would get the balance of $1,500,000?

In addition to the sale for cash, other options may have been considered:

a. Part cash payment; part stock, with Sanders to get, say, 49% interest in the new company. Although Sanders shied away from stock, he may, if he had consulted with others, have found this option desirable. It would have given him a share in the possible future success of the company and have given him capital gains which would have been taxable at the special rates at the time of the eventual resale of the firm.

b. A royalty arrangement, say 25% up to 50% of the franchise fees over the next five or ten years—or whatever time he continued to act as goodwill and P.R. man. This, too, would have given him a share in the future earnings.

c. A profit-sharing arrangement with profits to be distributed to Sanders over and above an agreed rate of return on capital of the new firm. Again, the time period could be set based on the time that Sanders would actively promote the company.

Some form of the royalty or profit-sharing arrangement could be combined with a payment of, say, $1,000,000 to satisfy Sanders' desire for cash in hand.

The price that Sanders set apparently came off the top of his head, since he commented, "I think that $2,000,000 sounds about right." If he had made any calculations, he may have figured that the current profits, estimated at $300,000, capitalized at 15% would come to $2 million. He apparently did not take into account the potential growth of the company. Even from 1960 to 1963, when he was running the company, estimated profits had grown from $100,000 to $300,000, which should have given him an inkling that future increases could be anticipated. Advice from a CPA, financial manager, or banker might have alerted him to make some provision for possible future gains even though the outlook at the time of the sale could not be predicted with any degree of accuracy.

In conclusion, it may be said that Sanders was a remarkably successful person. He was a great salesman and promoter, but he did not seek advice when got into an area outside of his own expertise.